BROKEN COMPASS
Finding Your Way Again after Divorce

VIVIAN RUSH

LUCIDBOOKS

Broken Compass
Finding Your Way Again after Divorce
Copyright © 2017 by Vivian Rush

Published by Lucid Books in Houston, TX.
www.LucidBooks.net

All rights reserved. No part of this publication may be reproduced, stored in a retrieval system, or transmitted in any form by any means, electronic, mechanical, photocopy, recording, or otherwise, without the prior permission of the publisher, except as provided for by USA copyright law.

Scripture taken from the New King James Version®. Copyright © 1982 by Thomas Nelson. Used by permission. All rights reserved.

ISBN-10: 1632961075
ISBN-13: 9781632961075
eISBN-10: 1632961083
eISBN-13: 9781632961082

Special Sales: Most Lucid Books titles are available in special quantity discounts. Custom imprinting or excerpting can also be done to fit special needs. Contact Lucid Books at info@lucidbooks.net.

In loving memory of my mother, Edna King, for all of the sacrifices she made as a single mom. She was small in stature, but one of the strongest women I ever knew. How she ever raised four kids all alone after Dad left, I'll never know. Her road was much tougher than anything I've had to face, but her example showed me how to live and love through the hard places of life and still keep my faith in God. Hers is still the voice in my head encouraging me and the face I long to see. Maybe some day soon, Mom. I love you.

TABLE OF CONTENTS

PREFACE 1

PART ONE: LOST IN THE FOG

Chapter 1: Letting Go 5

Chapter 2: Foothold in the Darkness 11

Chapter 3: Pushing through Guilt 19

PART TWO: THE FOG IS LIFTED

Chapter 4: A Bitter Root 31

Chapter 5: The Healing Oil of Joy 46

Chapter 6: Seeing through the Rain 60

Chapter 7: Islands Can Be Lonely 72

PART THREE: INCREASED VISIBILITY

Chapter 8: Out of Focus 83

Chapter 9: No Longer a Victim 95

Chapter 10: Follow the Path 107

PREFACE

"If your Bible is torn apart, your life is not." This was something that I wrote in the front of my Bible many years ago. I can't recall where the quote came from, nor can I remember who it was that said it. However, I know precisely the reason I wrote it. At the time, I had lost all sense of direction.

A little further down I also wrote, "Pain may be inevitable, but misery is optional." It is a fact that pain is very real to all of us at some point in our lives, and how we handle painful experiences is tied inevitably to whether God's Word is a pivotal part of our daily walk. His Word, if we stay in it long enough, brings joy and peace to us when we've been wounded. It's difficult to stay miserable when we practice hiding His words in our hearts, and if somehow we lose our way, His words can give us new direction!

My life changed suddenly and dramatically when my husband of twenty-six years left me. The Lord, through His Word, has pieced it back together again, but to be perfectly honest, it's a journey still in progress. It's a journey of letting go—of people, hurts, anger, fear, and most definitely some dreams that I held onto. It's also been a journey in finding a new path after being taken from the one I started on many years ago—something I had to do in order to walk into the future God has for me.

Instinctively when we lose something, we reach out to grasp something else. Sometimes we grasp for things that are not meant for us. Other times we try to hold onto what we have, even when it's obvious it's not for us anymore. I heard a pastor teaching many years ago about the fact that God is waiting for us all to go out into the deep with Him, but sometimes we allow circumstances, our past, and even people to hold us back. He said, "You can't discover new oceans until you're willing to lose sight of the shore!" I had been guilty of sitting on the beach, grasping at grains of sand sifting through my fingers, not willing to even get into the boat!

How true that is for most of us. Sometimes, we're not willing to let go of the things we've held dear for so long, even when it means moving on to something greater in our life! Some of us have even been guilty of staying in the same place (not just physically, but spiritually as well) even when it meant remaining miserable. We've opted for sameness because, hey, at least we're used to this! It's much scarier for us to launch out into unchartered territory.

I was not expecting to have to let go of anything—especially not my husband and my life as I'd known it for so long. For me, finding a new path was forced on me by the decision of someone else. At the age of forty-eight, after a quarter-century of being married to the same man, I found myself suddenly, painfully single. It became official on November 1, 2002, but not nearly as emotionally official to my already aching heart as when my ex-husband remarried only a month later. Perhaps that doesn't sound so bad to some, since divorce has become so accepted in our society that it's happening virtually every day to millions of people in our nation alone—but it was most truly a surprise when it happened to me.

I am one of an ever-shrinking number of people who happen to think marriage is supposed to last a lifetime; I imagine I feel so strongly because of the way divorce touched my family. My parents divorced when I was nine. I have friends and family members who have gone through divorces of their own. I've seen, firsthand, the devastation in the immediate family unit, as well as among other family members and friends.

But things happen that we neither plan for nor desire, and this is a book about a gracious Lord who meets us where we are, picks us up, dusts us off, and says, "Look only to me. I still have plans for you." I pray that this book will be an encouragement to anyone who has found herself in the middle of a situation (or situations) that seem overwhelmingly painful, and maybe even impossible. It's possible to find your way again after a divorce and to feel joy and peace even in the midst of the pain and turmoil. May God bless you as you read.

PART ONE
LOST IN THE FOG

Chapter 1
LETTING GO

"While we do not look at the things that are seen, but at the things which are not seen. For the things that are seen are temporary, but the things which are not seen are eternal."

—2 Cor. 4:18

It's just a camping trip, and you have everything you need. More than what you need, really, because you've done this more times than you can count. Preparation is key, you think, and as long as you've planned and packed sufficient equipment, nothing can go wrong. You don't even fear the dark, heavy sky above—a little rain can't deter you. Things have been busy lately, and you feel the need to get away.

Now you're getting ready for the deep, rejuvenating sleep only the mountains can offer. What could be better? This was just what you'd been waiting for. You've worked hard, and deserve this quiet time away from all the noise.

A few hours later, it's the middle of the night, and you're awakened suddenly by a loud clap of thunder and the rain pelting against your tent. You're startled, but you tell yourself that you've been through storms before and you might as well just try to get some sleep. But the rain only grows louder and heavier—you're surprised at the severity of it. As the moments pass you realize that this could be more than just a little rainstorm. You begin to wonder if you're prepared for this, and an uneasiness settles in.

Within moments, you're wide awake and truly afraid. What should you do? Where should you go? You feel the urgency to act, but can't decide what to do. The wind is threatening to rip your tent apart, and your mind races with the possibilities. The nearby river could flood; the tent could wash away; you can be seriously injured. How can you shield yourself from the elements at this point? Is it too late? You feel exposed and vulnerable. You need to move to higher ground, even if it is pitch black outside. Better safe than sorry. From the sound of the storm, time is of the essence. You need to act, but a numbness has come over you, and you feel unable to move.

Finally, you grab your poncho and pull on your boots with trembling hands. Finding your knapsack in the dark, you feel for your flashlight and leave the tent, but it's too late. You've waited too long.

A gust of wind knocks you off your feet and takes your breath away, loosening the flashlight from your grip. It rolls down the slope out of reach. This can't be happening! Fear has taken over now.

The river is rising, and you must make it to higher ground. It's your only chance for survival. You've never felt more helpless and alone.

～ ～ ～ ～

Life seemed simpler before May 2002 when my husband of nearly twenty-six years came home from work to tell me he was leaving me. Whether life was truly that good in years past or my memory has added a rosy filter, the fact remains that I occasionally find myself missing those familiar days when everything made sense, and when getting out of bed didn't take so much effort.

I knew on that morning in May that nothing would ever be the same again. The bed I'd slept in for years suddenly became a vast, empty stranger to me. I was suddenly and most definitely alone. Oh, I'd been alone in it before—my firefighter husband worked hours that caused him to be away at nights sometimes—but now I knew it was very possible that it would be permanently absent of him.

His clothes still hung in the closet, but even those disappeared within a matter of days. The feeling is still the same whether you lose a spouse to death or divorce—everything moves in slow motion. Either way, at this point of initial shock, most people are going through the motions numbly. It's almost like an out-of-body experience: you can see yourself dressing, eating, and going to work in your same routine except that nothing is familiar anymore and nothing feels normal.

It's as if someone is playing a terrible practical joke you'll never find humorous. I half expected to wake up and find it was all a bad dream. I prayed for that to be the case! But no matter how hard I prayed, I woke up each day to the same directionless emptiness. At the time, both of my children were living with me, as well as my then-eighteen-month-old grandson. When they were home, I held my emotions in check as best as I could so as not to upset them any more than they already were. They were suffering from the same shock I was. We were in a frozen state of breathlessness.

The need to know why became overwhelmingly important, and the answering silence seemed only to increase our pain.

After about a month, my son said, "Mom, I know this sounds crazy, but I think it would have been easier if he'd died." It didn't sound crazy to me at all. I knew exactly what he was talking about. If my husband had died, I would have at least had the comfort of knowing that when he left this earth, I was loved. The knowledge that all had been right with us at his passing would keep me going. The knowledge that we would be together again someday would be a very real hope in my heart. But I had neither of those things, nor did my children.

The man we knew was gone. Even now, as my children seek to have a relationship with their father, they know things will never be the same again. It's often inevitable with divorce—trust is broken; relationships are marred. You have nothing to hold onto.

I didn't want to let go. Everything within me cried out, "No! I won't move past this! This was my marriage!" I hoped that maybe, if I just held my breath long enough, he'd come to his senses and everything would go back to normal. I didn't get to the point of acceptance until the divorce itself became final. Somehow, reading those words in print, "It is hereby decreed . . . the marriage of . . . is dissolved," made it all real. I went home, sat in my chair, and bawled for hours. How could I be hurting this badly while he didn't feel any pain? How do you just turn your love off? I still loved him. How did this happen? When did this happen? How could I ever find my way?

In her book *Praying God's Word*, Beth Moore wrote, "The steps of the believer are steeped in constant change. Fingers are painfully peeled away from the security of sameness one at a time, again and again. Great wisdom lies in freeing our fellow sojourners . . . cherished though they are. With hands freshly loosed, we find liberty to embrace the One who will never change, and courage to release to Him those who ever will!"[1]

We all experience change, and change is often uncomfortable, often painful. But God will never leave us stranded. His love will never change, go away, and leave us hurting and bleeding on the inside. His is a love that can be counted on!

He is the one person we can count on. I may have landed in unfamiliar territory, but He is the King of unfamiliar territory too! He knows exactly where we are. He sees the curveballs before they ever come our way. He wants to meet us in whatever stage of hurt we are in.

The grief is real. The sense of loss is enormous. But with His help, even though the sadness will never completely go away, He helps us to let go of the grief.

---

1. Beth Moore, *Praying God's Word* (Nashville: B&H Publishing Group, 2009), 125.

Here are some Scriptures that I suggest highlighting. Even write them on cards and place them on your mirror in your bathroom, on your computer, wherever you can look at them throughout your day. That's what I did. It doesn't help to read them once and move on. When a heart is hurting, it needs to be reminded constantly.

> Unless the Lord had been my help, my soul would soon have settled in silence. If I say "my foot slips," your mercy, O Lord will hold me up.
>
> —Psa. 94:17, 18

> Cast all your cares on Him, for He cares for you.
>
> —1 Pet. 5:7

> The righteous cry out and the Lord hears, and delivers them out of all their troubles. The Lord is near to those who have a broken heart, and saves such as have a contrite spirit.
>
> —Psa. 34: 17, 18

> My grace is sufficient for you, for my strength is made perfect in weakness.
>
> —2 Cor. 12:9b

> You number my wanderings, put my tears into Your bottle; are they not in Your book? When I cry out to You, then my enemies will turn back; this I know because God is for me. . . . What can man do to me?
>
> —Psa. 56:8-11

> Peace I leave with you. My peace I give to you; not as the world gives, do I give to you. Let not your heart be troubled, neither let it be afraid.
>
> — John 14:27

You hold me by my right hand. You will guide me with your counsel, and afterward receive me to glory . . . whom have I in heaven but You . . . God is the strength of my heart and my portion forever.

—Psa. 73:23b-26

Cast your burden on the Lord, and He shall sustain you; He shall never permit the righteous to be moved.

—Psa. 55:22

I can do all things through Christ who strengthens me.

—Philip. 4:13

Weeping may endure for a night, but joy comes in the morning.

—Psa. 30:5b

You who have shown me great and severe troubles shall revive me again, and bring me up again from the depths of the earth. You shall increase my greatness and comfort me on every side.

—Psa. 71:20, 21

Then they cry out to the Lord in their trouble, and He brings them out of their distresses; he calms the storm so that the waves are still. Then they are glad because they are quiet; so He guides them to their desired haven.

—Psa. 107: 28-30

Though I walk in the midst of trouble, You will revive me; You will stretch out Your hand against the wrath of my enemies, and Your right hand will save me.

—Psa. 138: 7

Chapter 2
FOOTHOLD IN THE DARKNESS

> Then He arose and rebuked the wind, and said to the sea, "Peace, be still!" And the wind ceased and there was a great calm. But He said to them [his disciples], "Why are you so fearful? How is it that you have no faith?"
>
> —Mark 4:39, 40

It's amazing how a storm can make everything look different. Exhausted from a night of racing the river, now you're in the middle of nowhere, alone, with no idea what to do next. Your heart begins to race as you realize how far you are from civilization. You've lost your campsite and flashlight, and your knapsack is worse for wear. Last night seems like a blur, but the memory of the storm and what followed makes you shiver in response. You aren't sure what lies ahead, and again you begin to feel panicky. The thought of being lost in these woods brings no comfort.

The best thing to do is to come up with a plan. You've always prided yourself on your ability to think on your feet, so now would be a good time to practice. You take a few deep breaths to calm your nerves, and let your mind take the lead over your emotions. You can fix this. You know, at least, which direction you came from. That's obvious. You need only to walk the opposite direction from where the river was flowing to go in the direction of the campsite. But, how far might that be? You have no idea, because everything looks strange to you in the early morning light. If you could only find something familiar! You don't recognize this part of the woods. The trees are denser here, and there are no landmarks to jog your memory and help you find your bearings. You fear you'll never be able to locate your campsite.

As you sit on the bank of the river, a ripple of fear creeps through your chest. Never before have you felt that things were so out of your control. If only you could go back and start over, maybe you would've prepared better for something like this. You open your soggy knapsack to search the contents. The snacks are there. So are the maps, although drenched, and your compass. You pull it out to find your way, only to find it cracked and no longer working. Your cell phone, too, is waterlogged and won't turn on. Now you find it hard to hold fear at bay as you realize everything you were relying on to help you find your way is destroyed.

Soon you'll be lost in the dark.

~ ~ ~ ~

The first panic attack I had was one of the most uncomfortable things I've ever experienced. My heart was racing. Then I couldn't catch my breath, as if all of the air in the room had been sucked out. The walls were closing in on me. My chest began to ache as if someone had sat on it and wouldn't get off. If I'd been fully awake, I probably would have recognized it for what it was. However, I was still trying to struggle out of a deep, dream-filled sleep, so what was happening seemed too terrifying to me to recognize.

I called for my son, Ben, who was in the next room. I remember telling him my chest was hurting. For all I knew, I was having a heart attack. Then, I asked him to pray for me. His words told me he was much wiser than I had realized. He began, "Lord, touch my mom right now. Calm her fears. Give her peace. Help her to know you're with her, and she doesn't need to be afraid, Lord." He continued to pray for a few moments, and the feelings passed. God did calm my spirit.

It happened the night of my last real conversation with my ex-husband after yet another failed attempt to get his life back. It was December of 2003, a year since our divorce and his marriage to the woman he'd left me for. After he married her, it was as if a lightbulb finally turned on and he realized what he'd done. He had tried several times in that year to leave her, and there was talk of him getting his marriage to her annulled. Each time, he shared that he hoped to reconcile with me. Even so, he failed to free himself of the bondage he was in.

I had not gone right to sleep that night. Too much was going through my mind. More than anything, I was realizing that I had just witnessed what was probably going to be the last attempt my ex-husband made to reconcile with his family—or at least with me. I knew it would be, because I knew I wouldn't be able to allow it again. I had previously told someone that I had not been able to let go of him, because I hadn't felt the Lord let me release him yet. I felt it now—no question. It couldn't have been clearer if it had been in an audible voice.

He had gone a couple of months without seeing or talking to her, something he'd been counseled to do as she seemed to control him so much. Now she was back in his life again. I knew two things: she would never leave him alone, and God had never intended for me to subject myself to more pain, or to a life of wondering if he'd ever come back or not. After all our years together, I wouldn't settle for a halfhearted partner in life—certainly not a double-minded one who was constantly confused. I knew what marriage was supposed to be, and this wasn't it.

So my dreams that night were not sweet ones. They were troubled dreams, the kind filled with sadness, separation, and unknown, unseen, formidable enemies trying to snatch at me. You know, like being chased, or running away from someone and falling from a cliff—only you wake up just before you hit the ground.

It was fear. Fear had reared its ugly head and become real to me that night.

Fear is one of Christians' worst enemies. It can steal our joy and make us unwilling or unable to move in any direction. It can render us powerless and paralyzed if we don't recognize its presence and deal with it swiftly and with authority.

For several days, I allowed it to do that to me. All I wanted to do was lie in my bed, so that's just what I did—even when I recognized it for what it was. What was I afraid of? I was afraid of being alone. I was afraid of facing the future. I'd put so much effort into the whole idea of reconciliation, that now that all hope was lost of anything being "fixed," I was scared to face my life without it—without him. I didn't know how to do it. I didn't feel equipped to do it. But most of all, I didn't want to do it alone! I wanted to grow old with someone, not face the uncertainty of the rest of my life by myself. I had been married to my husband for more than half of my life; I hated to admit just how much I had come to depend on him. What would I do?

I allowed it to get to me in part because, quite honestly, I felt I deserved that. Isn't that the most idiotic thing you've ever heard? I deserved to be defeated? What kind of nonsense is that? Thankfully, the Lord does know our frame. His Word says, in Psalm 103:13-14, "As a father pities his children, so the Lord pities those who fear Him. For He knows our frame; He remembers that we are dust."

He remembered me in my grief. After Ben's prayer, He continued applying a healing balm on my fresh wounds. He spoke peace every time my wounded heart cried out, "It's not fair!" or "Why did you let me go down that road, God, if you knew what would happen?" It's just like the song that says, "Sometimes he calms the storm; other times he calms His child." He's quite capable of just stopping the storms from happening, but for reasons unknown to us, there are times he allows us to go through the storms, speaking words of peace and encouragement as we go through them. Either way, we need to remember He has our best interests at heart. We have such narrow vision, affected by what our limited, human perspective is; He sees the big picture.

We need to see things as He sees them and learn to trust that He knows what He's doing!

After those few days of complete misery, He finally gave me a breakthrough as I slowly got back to His Word. The breakthrough came, at first, through my memories.

It was as if He was showing me a video of all the happier times we'd had in the past, one memory at a time. I could see us young and in love again. I could see us when the kids were born and on vacations. I was reminded of family holidays together. Then, when the tape was through playing, I could almost hear someone say, "Those are the things Satan can't steal from you! You'll always have those memories—they won't go away. They're a part of who you are."

He also showed me that as good as memories can be, they are just that—memories. He reminded me that my life wasn't over, that He still has plans for me, and I'm not alone. God was now my best friend, my lover, my husband. And He would be better at all of those things than any man could ever be.

The opposite of fear is not boldness or courage; it's possible to be bold and courageous and still have fear in our hearts. No, I think the opposite of fear is faith! Faith, not in ourselves, but in a God who is bigger than our situations, other people, anything!

I've had to deal with some everyday issues that may seem mundane to most people, but to a woman who is still getting used to living on her own after years of having a husband to take care of her, life sometimes looms very heavily in front of me. This has caused some very real fear to come against me—especially fear of financial failure. The Lord has very graciously worked those things out, little-by-little, and sent some people my way to help me. He will do that for us, if we ask Him to, because He is concerned about every detail of our lives.

Fear will come against us. It's inevitable as long as we are living in this world, which can be a scary place if we aren't covering ourselves daily with the armor of God. Ephesians 6:13-18 discusses this armor we are to protect ourselves with. Yes, we are battling against principalities and powers of darkness. But listen to this text. Let it sink in. It will lift you up out of any fear that has shown up on your doorstep, seeking to not only come in, but take over your life.

It says in verses thirteen through eighteen:

> Therefore take up the whole armor of God that you may be able to withstand in the evil day, and having done all, to stand. Stand therefore, having girded your waist with truth, having put on the breastplate of righteousness, and having shod your feet with the preparation of the gospel of peace; above all, taking the shield of faith with which you will be able to quench all the fiery darts [and fear *is* one of those fiery darts the enemy hurls at us!] of the wicked one. And take the helmet of salvation, and the sword of the Spirit, which is the word of God; praying always with all prayer and supplication in the Spirit, being watchful to this end with all perseverance and supplication for all the saints.

Notice, the Word tells us to stand. When fear hits us, our first instinct is probably to run, which makes it very difficult to stand against our enemy! But we *have* to face our adversary—otherwise, we've already admitted defeat before we've even attempted to fight.

We also can't fight the enemy if we are sitting down or, worse yet, lying down! Of course, Ephesians is speaking of our mental, emotional, and spiritual stance. But think for a minute: when we get up in the morning, we don't try to get dressed sitting or lying down. We have to get up first!

Every piece of this armor is vital to success. You can't go "half dressed" into battle with the enemy of our souls—it would be spiritual suicide. Yet that's what many of us are guilty of. The times I feel the most defeated in this area of fear are when I haven't spent the time in His Word (the sword) as much as I should. Or maybe my faith (the shield) has been misplaced. Perhaps I've been trusting in myself or someone else more than in my God, who alone is able to protect my heart. Isn't that what a shield is important for? It's meant for protecting that vital organ that gives us life against the enemy's fiery darts meant to take that life! To battle the spirit of fear we must pray always, and in the Spirit. Romans 8:26-28 says:

> Likewise the Spirit also helps in our weaknesses. For we do not know what we should pray for as we ought, but the Spirit makes intercession for us with groanings that cannot be uttered . . . He who searches the heart knows what the mind of the Spirit is . . . He makes intercession for the saints according to the will of God . . . all things work together for good to those who love God, to those who are called according to His purpose.

He wants us to pray in the Spirit because, in those fearful times we face, He alone knows what it is that we need, and He makes intercession for us in those times! Wow! How powerful praying in the Spirit is! We can face anything through Him.

Since the Word of God is that sword of the Spirit, which is part of the armor of God, let me add some more Scriptures that deal with fear. Memorize them if you haven't already. Quote them daily, especially if fear is an area you need help in. They will bring you through if you bathe yourself in them and in prayer every day.

> For you did not receive the spirit of bondage again to fear, but you received the Spirit of adoption by whom we cry out, "Abba, Father."
> —Rom. 8:15

> Do not be afraid of sudden terror, nor of trouble from the wicked when it comes, for the Lord will be your confidence, and will keep your foot from being caught.
> —Prov. 3:25, 26

Be anxious for nothing; but in everything by prayer and supplication with thanksgiving, make your requests be known to God and the peace that passes all understanding will guard your hearts and minds in Christ Jesus.

—Philip. 4:6

Whenever I am afraid, I will trust in You. In God (I will praise His Word), In God I have put my trust . . . I will not fear. What can flesh do to me?

—Psa. 56:3, 4

In the fear of the Lord there is strong confidence, and His children will have a place of refuge.

—Prov. 14:26

For I, the Lord your God, will hold your right hand, saying to you, "Fear not, I will help you."

—Isa. 41:13

I sought the Lord, and He heard me, and delivered me from all my fears.

—Psa. 34:4

Fear not, for I have redeemed you; I have called you by your name; you are mine. When you pass through the waters, I will be with you; and through the rivers, they shall not overflow you. When you walk through the fire, you shall not be burned, nor shall the flame scorch you, for I am the Lord your God, the Holy One of Israel, your Savior.

—Isa. 43:1b-3a

Chapter 3
PUSHING THROUGH GUILT

> But one thing I do, forgetting those things which are behind and reaching forward to those things which are ahead, I press toward the goal for the prize of the upward call of God in Christ Jesus.
>
> —Philip. 3:13b, 14

"God, where are you?" you wonder out loud. God seems to be silent, and you consider this to be your own fault. Thoughts of past mistakes cloud your thinking now, and it's hard to hear His voice. The only voice you can make out is the one telling you that things could be different if only you'd made another choice about this trip, or your life. Accusing thoughts about mistakes that are now past correcting seem to be whispering your name. You shouldn't have come here. Once again, you've tried to take control of your life in your own independent way, and now you're paying for it.

Isn't that how it works? You do your best, so God gives you His. No, that didn't come out right. But you can't think clearly now, so you push thoughts and prayers aside and opt for one of the soggy granola bars from your knapsack. Not much of a supper, but it's better than nothing! Just another reason to be kicking yourself for your choices right now. If only you'd planned more for an emergency like this, you might have better options. But for now, the raisins, honey, and almonds are sweet and chewy, and you cling to every sensuous bite. Right now, you'll cling to anything.

Have you ever met someone who seems to be living in the past? They just don't ever seem to talk about anything except what used to be or what could have been, *if only*. I've met people like that—in fact, I was married to one of them. It may be because he was, and perhaps still is, a perfectionist. A true perfectionist is someone who has a difficult time accepting anything that is not "just right" in his own life, as well as in other people.

In the course of our marriage, he often began sentences with "I wish I would have" or "I should have." Any time he made a mistake in judgment or made a not-so-great choice or didn't follow through with something, it seemed he just could not get past it. I honestly think he was probably harder on himself than those of us around him. He just couldn't get over the fact that he made mistakes.

Imagine the torture he must have put himself through when he messed up our marriage! It wasn't until our divorce was final and he remarried that he saw the reality of what he'd done. What followed was a torturous year for all concerned as we watched him leave his circumstances at least three times, only to go back again, over and over. It was confusing for all of us—and painful beyond expression. The hardest part, though, was watching and knowing the toll it took on him.

Regrets will tell you all is lost. Regrets will tell you, "I've messed up so badly; how can I possibly fix this?" Regrets will beat you down to the point that you feel all hope of anything being right again is gone. Call it guilt, shame, remorse, even condemnation (which, by the way, comes only from the enemy of our souls)—whatever you choose to call it, it still feels the same. It yells in our faces that we're losers, that we cannot rise above whatever it is we've done. How could anyone forgive us, especially a holy and righteous Lord? It tells us we will never be anything in this life—we've lost it all.

We need to recognize it for what it is and who it came from. Only then can we deal with it as we should. I know what I'm talking about; I've been there, done that, many times in this process.

Regret, or guilt, is different from having conviction through the Holy Spirit about sins we've committed. Conviction doesn't point a finger at us. Conviction sheds light on our mistakes, yes, but it also points a finger straight to the cross. There, we can lay those sins and our burdens down at the feet of Jesus and ask for forgiveness. Scriptures tell us He will forgive us—and not only that, but He actually chooses to forget our sins. Psalm 103:12 says, "As far as the east is from the west, so far has He removed our transgressions from us." Conviction is good for us. Conviction doesn't put us down or make us feel all is lost. Instead it simply reveals the truth of God's Word in our hearts and shows us we need to make a change. Conviction brings about a peace that is possible only through the blood of Jesus, covering both the sin and the sinner.

Along with the anger I had toward my ex-husband over what he'd done to my life, his life, and our family, I had to deal with feeling guilty for my part in all of it. It was easier, actually, to forgive him than it was to forgive myself—after all, he was gone, but I had to live with myself every day! I had to look in the mirror every morning and every night, and I wasn't pleased with what I saw.

I wasn't under conviction; I was under condemnation. And it wasn't God who was my accuser; it was Satan. He's always the accuser. If he can't get us to feel bad about what we've done, he'll accuse us for what we didn't do. That's where I was. I couldn't get over the things I hadn't done:

"If you'd been a better wife, he wouldn't have looked somewhere else!"

"Why didn't you lose that weight you kept complaining about? If you'd done something with the way you look, he would have loved you!"

"Why didn't you agree with him about buying a new house when he brought it up?"

"Why did you keep nagging him about taking care of that situation?"

"Why didn't you warn him more strongly about that woman at work?"

"Why did you question him so much?"

"Why didn't you question him more?"

"Why didn't you show you appreciated him more?"

"Why did you have to sound so harsh with him?"

It seemed there was no end to the negative attacks on my character. I felt totally defeated as a woman, as his wife, and as a Christian. I'd blown it. Here I was with a marriage that had lasted twenty-six years, and I now had nothing to show for all the hard work we'd put into it.

The truth, of course, is that it takes two people to make a mess in a marriage. We both had done things that spelled potential disaster. It wasn't that I hadn't made mistakes; I truly had. But I was placing upon myself a burden that God never meant for me to carry! I was bombarded with all kinds of wrong thoughts. This wasn't from my merciful God—He knew my heart better than even I did. He knew the mistakes I'd made, but He also knew how badly I wanted my marriage to stay together.

We'd been through some tough times in our family. We had just helped our daughter through a very hard year-and-a-half. At seventeen, she had given birth to a child out of wedlock. The father denied having any part in it. Since it seemed a potentially abusive situation if we involved his family, she'd opted not to put his name on the birth certificate. It had been painful for her and painful for us to watch her go through. We had rallied around her as a family unit, and, I thought, made it through still intact as a family. We all adored Jordan, who was now a very important member of our household; he brought us so much joy that none of us could imagine life without him. We felt truly blessed, despite how it had all begun. God had seen us through.

Yet the end of one struggle had brought on another, one I hadn't expected. As parents, we suddenly found ourselves in a battle of wills that sometimes made us wonder why we had ever wanted to have children. I'm sure we weren't alone in those feelings as parents. I told a friend once that I think it must be necessary for parents to go through some battles with their kids as they reach adulthood, so that by the time they leave home, you're ready for them to go! (Not really, but it felt that way, at the time!) Whatever the case, it wasn't fun. Let's just say we were butting heads over the usual things parents deal with when they have teenagers—the only complication was, we now had a teenager with a child. That made it even harder.

The other problem was that we, as husband and wife, had a difference of opinion on how things should be handled. It was strange, actually—we'd always agreed on most parenting issues; now we seemed oceans apart. The things I felt should not have been ignored, he seemed to overlook; I found myself questioning him for what seemed to me his lack of concern or interest. (I realize now that at the time—which was probably six months or so before he left—he must have already been slipping away from me emotionally. That would explain the change.)

In addition to that, I was in the midst of menopause, but because of an earlier hysterectomy in my thirties, I didn't realize it. I had mood swings that kept me on the verge of tears almost daily. Sleep was rare. Irritability was constant. If I had known, would it have made a difference? Who knows? But now I was ripe for feelings of guilt and despair over the mistakes I'd made.

None of my negative thinking served any purpose. It didn't bring me victory over my situation. It didn't erase the fact that what happened was a done deal. It only served to make me what the enemy wanted me to be: a defeated Christian who was not only unwilling, but also unable, to stand up and walk victoriously into whatever life my Lord now was calling me into. I was so stuck on replaying every wrong decision that I couldn't move beyond it. I couldn't enter the life of peace and joy that only comes from knowing everything will work out for my good, if I forgive and choose to move forward.

The Lord began to deal with my heart about these feelings of regret and despair, and every time these negative, condemning thoughts came to me, I began to consciously say (either out loud or in my head):

> No. I won't accept that negative thought anymore. Lord, in Jesus name, take into captivity every thought in my mind, today. Tear down any false reasoning that would keep me from seeing Your truth in my life. I choose to thank You, Lord, despite what's happened in my life. Yes, I made mistakes, but I've asked for forgiveness for them, and You don't want me to stay bound by them, Jesus. I choose to believe You can take even my mistakes and turn them around for my good. You know my heart, Jesus. Thank you for what You will do in my life today.

Once I started doing that, the Lord began to open His Word once again to me. It's hard to hear His voice if we're so hung up on beating ourselves up, but by giving Him praise instead of constantly whining over what we've lost, we untie His mighty hands to do what He always could do. Guilt, regret, and condemnation emphasize how we as humans have failed, and we mistakenly think we are the ones who have to go back and fix everything. That's not God's way. He wants us to get our hands—and our thinking—out of it. The point He makes to us is that we can't do anything about it ourselves if we want to. His desire is to lift us up above the circumstances, so we can keep praising Him, and watch Him take over where we've messed up.

In *Praying God's Word*, Beth Moore talks about this very issue of having a stronghold amid your guilt. She writes:

> When fitted with the armor of God, we will not be blindsided by the fiery darts of the Enemy. Past failures lose their power, for they have been dealt with. Present thoughts will not overrun me, for I am in command of my thoughts and I make the final decision on what I believe. The opinions of others do not bombard me, for I

have decided to believe what God says about who I am—regardless of what I or anyone else thinks.[2]

In other words, God loves us and thinks we're worthwhile even though we've been (let's be honest here) pretty stupid at different times in our lives.

Moore also offers this truth from Romans 3:4: "Let God be true, though every man be found a liar." She goes on to say, "The only One who has a right to shape our lives is Jesus Christ. We must determine to allow nothing and no one to shape us, not even our personal experiences, unless they are consistent with the promises of God. In truth, who is ruling our lives, God, or our experiences?"[3]

Let's face it: we're not perfect. If we were, there'd be no reason for a Savior! None of us have "arrived." And since we've come to the conclusion that no one is perfect, let's also decide that the worst thing we can do in our Christian walk is to live by our emotions. When we mess up, and we most definitely will, we can't give up the fight just because we "feel" bad about something we did. Even our emotions can be wrong! We need to grasp the reality of who we are in Christ—period. Despite our frailty, God is more than able. His Word tells us that in our weakness, He is strong!

In 1 Corinthians 13:12 it says, "For now we see in a mirror dimly; but then [when we are finally with Him] face to face; now I know in part, but then I shall know just as I also am known." We need to filter our thoughts, feelings, and actions by faith, as God sees them. That's the key. It is a key that will finally unlock the door to a more joyful, peaceful walk, even through the storms and trials of this life. And, even when we make mistakes, we must turn them over to Him. Only then will we be free to move forward.

---

2. Beth Moore, *Praying God's Word* (Nashville, B&H Publishing Group, 2009), 146.
3. Ibid., 313.

These are some Scriptures that helped me to finally let go of the guilt that kept me trapped in my past, reliving over and over things that happened that I couldn't do anything about now. I learned with God's help that regrets and feeling guilty all the time can become a stronghold that keeps us from ever moving forward into a fulfilling, God-centered, victorious future. These Scriptures point to a forgiving Lord who is more than able to cover our mistakes, make up for them, and bless us despite them.

> Blessed are those whose lawless deeds are forgiven, and whose sins are covered.
>
> —Rom. 4:7

> Let us draw near with a true heart in full assurance of faith, having our hearts sprinkled from an evil conscience and our bodies washed with pure water. Let us hold fast the confession of our hope without wavering, for He who promised is faithful.
>
> —Heb. 10:22, 23

> "No weapon formed against you shall prosper, and every tongue [even our own!] which rises against you in judgment [condemnation] you shall condemn. This is the heritage of the servants of the Lord, and their righteousness is from me [notice, it's not our own self-righteousness]," says the Lord.
>
> —Isa. 54:17

> And we know that all things work together for good to those who love God, to those who are called according to His purpose.
>
> —Rom. 8:28

> Do not fret—it only causes harm.
>
> —Psa. 37:8b

All we like sheep have gone astray; we have turned, every one, to his own way; and the Lord has laid on Him the iniquity of us all.

—Isa. 53:6

There is therefore now no condemnation to those who are in Christ Jesus, who do not walk according to the flesh, but according to the Spirit.

—Rom. 8:1

The Lord will perfect that which concerns me. [To me, this implies that even though we're sure to mess things up as long as we live on this earth, He is more than able to take us and our imperfect ways and turn things around, if we submit our lives completely to Him!]

—Psa. 138:8a

And He said to me, "My grace is sufficient for you, for My strength is made perfect in weakness."

—2 Cor. 12:9a

Then they cried out to the Lord in their trouble, and He saved them out of their distresses; He brought them out of darkness and the shadow of death, and broke their chains in pieces.

—Psa. 107:13, 14

It is better to take refuge in the Lord than to trust in man [even myself!].

—Psa. 118:8

Who shall bring a charge against God's elect? It is God who justifies. Who is he who condemns? It is Christ who died, and furthermore is also risen, who is even at the right hand of God, who also makes intercession for us.

Who shall separate us from the love of God which is Christ Jesus our Lord? As it is written, "For Your sake we are killed all day long; we are accounted as sheep for the slaughter." Yet in all these things we are more than conquerors through Him who loved us, for I am persuaded that neither death nor life, nor angels nor principalities nor powers, nor things present nor things to come [and might I add things from our *past*], nor height nor depth, nor any other created thing, shall separate us from the love of God which is in Christ Jesus our Lord.

—Rom. 8:33-39

PART TWO
THE FOG IS LIFTED

Chapter 4

A BITTER ROOT

And do not grieve the Holy Spirit of God, by whom you were sealed for the day of redemption. Let all bitterness, wrath, anger, clamor and evil speaking be put away from you, with all malice.

—Eph. 4:30, 31

You wake up with a pounding in your head that tells of your rough, almost sleepless night on the damp ground. You hope that the sun will soon warm you. What you wouldn't give for a nice, hot cup of coffee right now! Anything to bring you comfort and calm your nerves.

How is it possible that you, of all people, feel this lost? You feel helpless and out of control. That is the problem: you've always needed control. Chalk it up to a childhood of moving around from place to place and never knowing what might happen next—and your present circumstances only make those feelings resurface. Now you feel something else rising up in you. Something even more disturbing than fear or even regret. You feel its effects even before you recognize it for what it is.

You're more than scared now. Now you're downright angry— angry at yourself for being so irresponsible in coming here alone! What were you thinking when you dropped everything and came up here without telling anyone? You kick the pile of branches beneath your feet. You'd kick yourself if you could. It might not relieve the pounding in your head, but it might relieve the building tension you feel.

And you realize that more than yourself, you're angry with God. Isn't He supposed to be a loving God? Doesn't He care that you're stranded on a mountain and left to die? Where is He now? Worst of all, you know that He is watching over this whole scenario, maybe even causing it to punish you some way. It's not fair! What were you supposed to do? How can you fight against God? You feel completely undone. Why doesn't He just help you out of this mess instead of standing by and watching you flounder around?

Your head is spinning now, and not just from lack of morning coffee. You know that this anger isn't resolving your current situation or helping you come up with a plan. It certainly isn't making you feel any better. On an empty stomach, all this soul-searching stuff is too much. You pull out another granola bar and head farther downstream.

⚘ ⚘ ⚘ ⚘

Anger can be the downfall of any believer, no matter how strong a Christian she is, when bitterness begins to take root. Psalm 4:4a says, "Be angry, and do not sin." I used to think that was a strange Scripture. First of all, it almost sounds like the Lord is giving us the go-ahead to do what I always had thought was a sin—to be angry. And second, it turns around and tells us not to sin! What's up with that? Well, I finally got it.

As His Word says, the Lord knows our frame. He knows we are only flesh and blood. There's not a person alive who doesn't get or hasn't gotten angry at some point! Even some of the meekest, mildest-mannered people on earth get angry sometimes. People may not say or do anything to vent their anger, but it's there. Interestingly, psychologists tell us that those who don't show their anger and hold their feelings in are often harmed physically more than the rest of us who let it out.

Didn't Christ Himself get angry at the moneychangers in the temple? Not only was He angry, but He drove them out of the temple. Not only did He drive them out, but He overturned their tables and the seats of those who sold doves! He went on to teach against what they were doing, saying, "Is it not written, 'My house shall be called a house of prayer for all nations'? But you have made it a den of thieves!" (Mark 11:17b).

That sounds like some good, old-fashioned anger to me, doesn't it to you? He physically showed He was angry when he overturned the tables. What's the difference between that and sinning because of anger? Here it is: Jesus didn't kill the moneychangers. He didn't raise a hand to even strike them. Because He was who He was, and the temple, after all, is a symbol of Christ's body, He had every God-given right to show His anger. He's God the Son; He was simply exerting His authority over them. But His desire was not to hurt those people—He just wanted them to see the truth!

I'm just as sure that Jesus hated what they were doing, but He separated that hate from the love he had for the moneychangers themselves. His Word is filled with the truth that Jesus loves the sinner but hates the sin. That's why I can say, with a great deal of confidence, that He loves me even when I sin. He has compassion for me, but He hates my sins. As Christians, we are to strive to be like Him, but it takes a lot of effort on our part not to lash out and do things in anger when our blood is boiling.

The minute the numbness wore off after my husband left, the fear set in—and once the fear was under control, then anger showed up on the scene. So many times in those first few years after my husband left me, I longed to have a live person in front of me that I could vent at! I often thought that I should've invested in one of those punching bags that boxers practice on.

By the end of July 2002, after having been alone for two months with no answers to my questions, I wrote these words in my journal:

> I seem to be able to handle each day a little better. I move forward and seem to get things done, while preparing myself for whatever might happen next. My confusion has turned to anger now. I just can't make up my mind whom I'm angry at the most—my husband, myself (for not being able to see this coming, and thus perhaps stop it!), the other woman, or the devil!

I remember being angry because, for one thing, here I was reaching menopause, and he didn't even have the decency to stick with me through it! I wrote, "Just because I'm probably looking older, maybe not as 'appealing' as he used to think I was, did he turn to someone he thought was more exciting? How dare he! He's no spring chicken either! Right now, I'm so angry at him for letting go of me; for letting go of us! Why? Why!"

I was reminded of a time, years ago, when he had been through a very hard time physically. It was back in 1992, exactly ten years before he left. It had started with an accident on the job. He'd been at a fire, and a porch roof had collapsed on him. He wasn't burned, but began having neck and back pain that got increasingly worse.

Eventually, he decided to go have a steroid shot in his spine. I'll never forget what happened that day: just before they came to take him for the shot, he looked at me and said, "I have a bad feeling about this." But before I could respond, "Maybe you shouldn't go through with it," it was time for him to go. He got the shot. At first, things seemed to go all right, but within a week, he had developed flu-like symptoms. He became as weak as a newborn puppy.

He'd always been so strong and athletic. He had seemed invincible as a younger man; he had been able to do anything he wanted. How could this have been happening to him? I remember the uneasy question that neither of us was able to put into words for a very long while: could it be cancer?

Doctor after doctor found nothing wrong that they could put their finger on. None could admit that a shot like the one he'd had could cause such severe problems. Most of them insinuated it was all in his head. One even suggested that he should take an HIV test! It was six months or a year later before we had the answer to what this sudden mysterious illness was: fibromyalgia—chronic pain. It is in the family of arthritis, chronic fatigue syndrome, and lupus. Usually it is brought on by trauma, either physical or emotional. There was no specific test to find it, or at least there wasn't at the time—it was found by process of elimination in taking tests of all different kinds for all other types of diseases.

It had taken so long to finally find our answer. Meanwhile, week after week, he had gone forward for prayer at church. We both believed God could perform a miracle. We stood together, believing. After a while, just not knowing what was happening to his body had worn him down emotionally, just as his body seemed worn down. I believe he was battling depression—who wouldn't be?

I wish I could say that the diagnosis was the end to our worries. But it wasn't. Finding just the right medicine to treat it and just the right dosage became almost as frustrating. Eventually, after a year and a half from the day of that shot, he was back on the road to recovery. It had taken its toll on him, but he'd made it to the other side of this crisis. We'd made it, together. I remember saying, jokingly, after we'd finally made it through all of that, "You know, after this, you absolutely cannot have a midlife crisis! This ought to count as one, so you won't have to, OK?" We'd laughed about it back then. It wasn't so funny to me now.

Now anger got a good grip on me. I'd seen him through all of that. I wanted to scream it at him: "I saw you through one of the hardest times of our marriage, and this is the thanks I get?" It would have been a valid accusation. Most people, I'm sure, would not have faulted me for feeling the way that I did.

Even the Scriptures seemed to agree with me. It was around this time that I highlighted this passage in my Bible, Psalm 35:12-15:

> They reward me evil for good, to the sorrow of my soul. But as for me, when they were sick, my clothing was sackcloth; I humbled myself with fasting . . . I paced about as though he were my friend or brother [try husband!]; I bowed down heavily, as one who mourns for his mother. But in my adversity, they rejoiced and gathered together . . . and I did not know it; they tore at me and did not cease.

When I came across that Scripture, I felt I couldn't have worded it any better.

David wrote this Psalm, possibly at a time when he was being hunted by King Saul, who sought to kill him out of jealousy—yet David loved him. He wanted the best for Saul. He'd served him loyally even when Saul hated him the most; even when he'd had the chance to harm Saul, he hadn't. He'd played music for Saul when Saul needed his spirits lifted up. He had always been there for him, yet Saul still sought to kill him.

Although our circumstances were quite different in many ways (my husband wasn't trying to kill me, and we'd had a mutual, faithful love for each other for twenty-five years of our twenty-six-year marriage), the feelings he'd expressed in those verses were much like the ones I was feeling. He felt betrayed, and so did I. He was hurting, and so was I. He'd done everything he could for Saul's good in a time when Saul needed him, and I had done the same for my husband. Didn't I have the right to be angry?

I asked myself this over and over.

Later, when I found out another woman, who professed to be a Christian, had deceived, lied, and encouraged my husband to leave me, these words in Psalm 94:4-7 hit the nail right on the head:

> They utter speech, and speak insolent things; all workers of iniquity [can't even so-called "Christians" be guilty of being workers of iniquity?] boast in themselves. They break in pieces your people, O Lord, and afflict your heritage. They slay the widow and the stranger, and murder the fatherless, yet they say, "The Lord does not see, nor does the God of Jacob understand."

Yet our promise comes later in the same Psalm, where it says, "Blessed is the man whom You instruct, O Lord, and teach out of Your law, that you may give him rest from the days of adversity, until the pit is dug for the wicked." Then in verses seventeen and eighteen: "Unless the Lord had been my help, my soul would soon have settled in silence. If I say, 'My foot slips,' Your mercy, O Lord, will hold me up."

You see, all of this anger was only serving to hurt me. Not him. Not her. That's what anger does. It takes so much of our energy, yet what we get in return is more grief—not joy. It affects us physically, causing higher blood pressure and ulcers. It affects our minds because we become obsessed with the person we're angry at. It affects us emotionally because it leaves us so unhappy and exhausted (because being mad is hard work!) that we have no room for the people who really need and deserve our attention.

My kids needed me to be there for them. So did my grandson. But I was so full of anger that I was snapping at everyone. The anger I felt for him definitely affected the way I treated my daughter, because she had to live with me. (My son had moved out on his own, so she, unfortunately, caught the brunt of my anger.) I remember her telling me that I didn't always have to take things out on her. She was right, of course.

The anger itself wasn't a sin. We're only being human when we feel anger. What I was doing with the anger was going to become sin, if I didn't get it together.

The first thing the Lord did in me was to help me see that the focus of my anger was on the wrong thing—or should I say the wrong person? I had to pray for Him to show me this; it didn't just come to me. My anger, up until now, was against my husband, and honestly, it was misplaced. God began to show me that I wasn't going to be set free from anger until I realized what had caused my husband to do the things he had done. It took a while to get there.

He began to show me that the way my husband was acting and reacting to things was very untypical of him. He had always been a family man, but suddenly, he was extremely absorbed in himself and in what he wanted. He'd always put our needs before his. He'd adored our grandchild (we had started calling Jordan "Papaw's boy" because they were so fond of each other); now he didn't even seem important to him. He didn't attempt to talk to the kids at all. He kept his cell phone turned off. Most of the time he even ignored their messages and wouldn't return their calls for days. This was so unlike him. Whenever I spoke to him, he was distant, uncaring, unsympathetic, and even mean in his treatment of me. I suddenly didn't know this man that for years had been my best friend.

Little-by-little, I was seeing that the real enemy here was not my husband—it was Satan. Obviously, there had been a lie (or perhaps many lies) that he had told my husband, and eventually he must have bought into them. This had slowly-but-surely caused him to see me as the enemy.

Just as clearly as I had felt anger, I knew that it had been anger that eventually turned into bitterness toward my husband. The bitterness had then taken root in his heart and had grown into a viny weed that choked out the love he had for me. This was Satan's work. No doubt about it. When I finally realized it, God could help me to see my husband in a different light. Now that the anger was directed at the right person (Satan), I could see my husband as the deceived victim, not the attacker! This was very important if the Lord was going to free me from the potential of becoming bitter and falling into sin myself.

What happened next I will never forget. You've probably heard of people confronting loved ones who are trapped in addiction, in hopes of startling them into facing their addiction and hopefully doing something about it. It was just that sort of intervention that God made in my life at this point. No, I wasn't an addict, but He knew I needed Him to get ahold of my mind, my emotions, and my very spirit, and make me see things clearly—once and for all.

On a Sunday morning, four months after my husband left me, God met me at the altar of my church in a way I'd never experienced Him before. God knows exactly what we need, and I needed to be prostrate before His throne. I won't tell you I heard Him speak audibly—I didn't. All I know is that I felt such peace as I lay there that I was in no hurry to leave. All I wanted to do was say His name, Jesus, over and over. I remember praising that name that was bigger than my problems, bigger than my hurts, and even bigger than the anger that I'd held inside of me. When I left that altar, I had a different perspective.

It was after that experience that I sat down and composed a letter to my husband. I had no idea when I would give it to him; I just knew I had to write it. It was what the Lord wanted me to do. I can't recall much of what I wrote. I told him that I was sorry for whatever I had done that had caused him to become so angry at me that he wanted to end our marriage. I spoke of how I still loved him, despite everything.

My daughter was the one to give it to him when he came by the house one day. She told him, seeing that he didn't act too interested in reading it, that she wanted him to read it through later. I assume he did, but I'm not sure, even now. I didn't necessarily expect it to change the course of events, although, admittedly, I wished for that to happen. It didn't. Nothing changed. He gave me no response, either in person or by letter. I could've been upset by that, but I wasn't, really. The letter was as much for me as it was for him. I hoped it would end any bitterness he had in his heart toward me, but I was also trying to lay down my anger toward him in hopes of preventing that bitterness to take root in my own heart—call it preventative medicine.

We have absolutely no control over what other people do. All we can do is make sure we take care and guard our own hearts against the enemy's schemes. He'd already caused havoc in my husband's life through anger and bitterness; now he sought to do the same in me and in our children. He's still attempting it at times. The Lord couldn't work to restore our marriage at all unless this was dealt with. I did my part, as best as I knew how, from that day on, to speak peace toward my husband every chance I got. It was up to him to do the same, if he was willing. I couldn't have done it without that time with Him at that altar. (By the way, it doesn't even have to be at an altar. He can speak to us in our home, in our car, at work. Wherever and whenever we submit our wills to Him, He will meet us.)

I'd like to share one more thing about this anger that we need to keep from our Christian walk. I was listening to a sermon that Joel Osteen of Lakewood Church here in Houston preached that first summer after my husband left. The name of his sermon was "Living a Life of Forgiveness." It fits in so well that I think it's worth sharing. I wrote some notes in my journal about it so I wouldn't forget the lesson he taught.

He said that bitterness and anger are like toxic waste that's been buried inside us. Eventually it will leak out, come to the surface, and contaminate our lives (this is also true of depression, low self-esteem, etc.). Osteen said:

> We're cramming all this unforgiveness, all this bitterness in there, into these big barrels, and we seal the lid and then we bury it as deep as we possibly can. And we think, good, now we're not going to have to deal with it. Took

care of that problem. Unfortunately, just like that toxic waste, it's going to come back to resurface and it's going to leak out. What does this toxic waste look like when it comes out in our lives? How is it displayed? In some people, it's simply anger.[4]

Another thing we do is put up walls, mistakenly thinking we're protecting ourselves from hurt. When we do this, we're actually keeping ourselves from reaching out to others, and we're not letting God work through us.

I couldn't say it any better than that! I can't help but be reminded of my mother. She was forty-six when my dad left us—two years younger than I was when my husband left—and she lived to be almost eighty. You couldn't find a woman with stronger beliefs than she had. She is the main reason I serve the Lord today—her example meant more to me than she could ever have imagined. However, I believe she never got past the hurt and bitterness she felt after my dad left. I'm not sure she was even aware of it, but I think she put walls around her heart after their divorce. She said she'd never trust another man. I don't blame her. Her pain had to have been a hundred times worse than mine. At least I'd had a faithful husband for a quarter of a century before the change took place. She had to live with my dad's unfaithfulness for seventeen years.

I think (and perhaps others who knew her would agree with me) that she lived with depression, fear, and low self-esteem as well. But the hidden bitterness came out in never really letting others get close to her from that point on—her family, maybe, but no one outside of it. She'd built an impenetrable wall, thinking she was protecting herself. She still was a wonderful Christian lady, but she let what happened stop her from living in His fullness as He intended her to—as He intends us all to do.

---

4. Joel Osteen, "Living a Life of Forgiveness," Lakewood Church, Houston, TX, March 5, 2000.

I don't want to just "survive" this. I want to be a stronger person because of it. That's God's purpose for all of us. Let me quote Joel Osteen one more time. In *Your Best Life Now*, he says that many who have been hurt by others are missing out on their "new beginnings" because they keep opening old wounds. We're still hanging onto our "ashes"—what's left of our dreams. Sometimes, like it or not, God wants us to lay those ashes down at the altar and stop mourning over something we have no control over. Sometimes, those ashes will cause us to be angry and bitter. Osteen writes, "You will have to rise up and say 'I don't care how disappointed I am, I'm not going to let this get the best of me. I'm moving on with my life.'" His advice is to "quit wasting time trying to figure out something you can't change. You can't unscramble eggs. What's done is done."[5]

We need to let God right the wrongs done to us in our lives. God knows where we are. He sees the hurts people have caused us, and He will pay us back for those wrongs. In fact, He promises that He will give us double for everything that's been taken away from us. Imagine that! But even if He doesn't, there is healing that we receive from releasing those who've hurt us to Him. He won't allow us to be continually hurt by someone. He will eventually put an end to the situation if we let Him work in it. Our job is to sit back and let Him vindicate us. Too many times, we try to do it ourselves and only end up frustrated and miserable.

I may not like what happened with my husband. I may not like what another woman allowed Satan to use her to do to my family. But God won't let me have any slack in this area. He will continue to work on me until I harbor no anger or bitterness against either one of them. As recently as this summer, fourteen years after the divorce, God laid it on my heart to pray for my ex-husband and his wife. I have to admit that I questioned Him about it at first. "Why? Why do I need to pray for them? I'm

---

5. Joel Osteen, *Your Best Life Now* (New York: Hachette Book Group, 2004), 175.

good!" I told Him. But He showed me that I still felt some resentment over something that I wasn't even aware of. It was as if He said, "Get rid of the seed of bitterness even before it becomes a root!" Since then, I make it a point to pray for both of them every day. I pray for God to reveal areas where they may still need healing. I pray for my children's relationship with their father. I declare I've forgiven them, and lay down any lingering anger and resentment. As I do this, God is changing me and giving me such peace!

Let's lay our anger down right now and every time it threatens to come up again, so that He can trade those ashes in for a life of peace and fulfillment in Him.

Here are some Scriptures that the Lord has given me over the years that have helped me in dealing with this:

> Pursue peace with all people, and holiness, without which no one will see the Lord; looking carefully lest anyone fall short of the grace of God; lest any root of bitterness springing up cause trouble, and by this many become defiled.
> —Heb. 12:14, 15

> Search me, O God, and know my heart; try me, and know my anxieties; and see if there is any wicked way in me, and lead me in the way everlasting.
> —Psa. 139:23, 24

> Be angry and do not sin; do not let the sun go down on your wrath, nor give place to the devil.
> —Eph. 4:26, 27

> But if you do not forgive men their trespasses, neither will your Father forgive your trespasses.
> —Matt. 6:15

And a servant of the Lord must not quarrel, but be gentle to all, able to teach, patient in humility correcting those who are in opposition, if God perhaps will grant them repentance, so they may know the truth, and they may come to their senses and escape the snare of the devil, having been taken captive by him, to do his will.

—2 Tim. 2:24-26

Let every man be swift to hear, slow to speak, slow to wrath; for the wrath of man does not produce the righteousness of God.

—Jam. 1:19b-20

And let the peace of God rule in your hearts, to which also you were called in one body; and be thankful.

—Col. 3:15

But if you have bitter envy and self-seeking in your hearts, do not boast and lie against the truth. This wisdom does not descend from above, but is earthly, sensual, and demonic. For where envy and self-seeking exist, confusion and every evil thing are there. But the wisdom that is from above is first pure, then peaceable, gentle, willing to yield, full of mercy and good fruits, without partiality and without hypocrisy. Now the fruit of righteousness is sown in peace by those who make peace.

—Jam. 3:14-18

A fool vents all his feelings, but a wise man holds them back.

—Prov. 29:11

Repay no one evil for evil. Have regard for good things in the sight of all men. If it is possible, as much as depends on you, live peaceably with all men. Beloved, do not avenge yourselves, but rather give place to wrath; for it is written, "Vengeance is Mine, I will repay," says the Lord. Therefore, "If your enemy is hungry, feed him; if he is thirsty, give him a drink; for in so doing, you will heap coals of fire on his head." Do not be overcome by evil, but overcome evil with good.

—Rom. 12:17-21

For we know Him who said, "'Vengeance is Mine. I will repay,' says the Lord." And again, "The Lord will judge His people."

—Heb. 10:30

In regard to the Lord's anger, listen to what the Bible shows us:

The Lord is merciful and gracious, slow to anger, and abounding in mercy. He will not always strive with us, nor will He keep His anger forever. He has not dealt with us according to our sins, nor punished us according to our iniquities. [In other words, He forgives us, even when we deserve punishment!]

—Psa. 103:8-10

For His anger is but for a moment, His favor is for life.

—Psa. 30:5a

For I know that You are a gracious and merciful God, slow to anger and abundant in lovingkindness, One who relents from doing harm.

—Jon. 4:2b

Chapter 5
THE HEALING OIL OF JOY

Weeping may endure for a night, But joy comes in the morning.
—Psa. 30:5

    You've started wondering how long it will be before anyone notices your absence. You start wondering if they'll even care—if God is OK with stranding you in the wilderness, maybe your family is too. Maybe nothing about your life was ever as good as it seemed before now. Was it ever good, or were you just kidding yourself? Maybe the life you've built for yourself is nothing more than a mirage. Maybe you fooled yourself, but was anyone else fooled? You ask yourself if there's anything redeemable in it at all. You don't seem to have an answer for that. You feel like a bundle of emotions, and tears threaten to erupt at any moment. It hurts to think that no one will care about what happens to you or even know if you get hurt or die out here. You begin to sense your need for someone—anyone—to care. Really care. You long for another person to wrap his or her arms around you and shield you from all of this. You have a feeling it's not just your present situation you want shielding from.

    At that moment, as you're wobbling through a particularly rocky part of the trail, you trip and stumble on a large rock partially hidden by the brush, and you fall flat on your stomach in the middle of the path. You felt your ankle give way in the fall, and you know immediately you've twisted it badly, or worse yet, sprained or broken it. Great! This is just what you need right now. Can it get any worse? You're not sure how you can go on.

🙢 🙢 🙢 🙢

I hope you have reached that "morning" that the Scripture text is speaking of. On the other hand, you may think you won't feel that joy again until Christ's return, or until He calls you home. But I do believe it's possible to reach a point in our journey, even through hurts and pain, where we can express joy despite the things we're experiencing. The Merriam-Webster dictionary defines *joy* as "the emotion evoked by well-being, success, or good fortune or by the prospect of possessing what one desires; the expression or exhibition of such emotion." In his article "How Do You Define Joy?" John Piper makes a distinction between the meaning of joy in general and Christian joy. He says, "Christian joy is a good feeling in the soul, produced by the Holy Spirit, as he causes us to see the beauty of Christ in the word and in the world."[6]

I might not always see the beauty of Christ in every circumstance, but I do get pleasure from the biblical expectation that these present things are temporary. I know beyond a shadow of a doubt that my future is bright as long as I have faith in a God who cares for my hurts. I get great satisfaction in my relationship with Christ, even when other relationships are sometimes cloudy at best, if not impossible! He gives me delight. He makes my heart glad. Even on some of my darkest days, when I've laid my heart before Him and sought His presence in prayer and in His Word, I've never walked away feeling empty.

---

6. John Piper, "How Do You Define Joy?" Desiring God, accessed July 25, 2015, http://www.desiringgod.org/articles/how-do-you-define-joy.

Jeremiah 29:11 says, "'For I know the plans I have for you,' declares the Lord, 'plans to prosper you, and not to harm you, plans to give you a hope and a future'" (NIV). The NKJV says it like this: "'I know the thoughts that I think toward you,' says the Lord, 'thoughts of peace and not of evil, to give you a future and a hope.'" You see, no matter what we're facing, what really matters is that we serve a God who's interested in our future. He plans for it to be full of peace. We are to hope for a brighter tomorrow. It's there for us to receive. However, it's up to us to reach up to Him and take this free gift. He already paid the price for it.

Sometimes, in order to be able to do that, we have to see past some very real hurts. That hurt can scream at us for attention. It is a voice that has to be reckoned with, demanding we not ignore it. To deny that it's there would be lying. Emotional hurts are not unlike injuries to our physical bodies. To just put Band-Aids on them and try to keep going without addressing the infection is asking for more trouble later on.

I knew of someone at work who jammed her finger pretty severely, making it swollen and painful to use. She was so afraid of what the doctor might have to do to fix it that she chose to just wrap it and go on, hoping that it would heal on its own. It didn't. Eventually she ended up going to the doctor anyway, but because she'd procrastinated, it became an even worse experience to get the finger to heal. Neglect had caused her even more trouble. It wasn't just jammed—it was broken. And because of the wait, it began to heal crooked. What she thought would heal on its own became an injury that caused her constant, unnecessary discomfort.

We can be like that when someone hurts us. What he or she did to us may be the most painful thing we've ever endured. You may have been hurt by someone else in your family. Maybe it was your daughter or son. Perhaps it was a parent. Or, it could've been a coworker, or even your boss. Maybe you were overlooked for a great promotion. It could be something relatively small or excruciatingly large. Whatever the hurt was, unless we get to the core of that wound and doctor it properly through prayer and whatever

God requires of us to do, it will never completely be healed.

People seem to handle pain and hurt in three different ways. There may be varying degrees of each one, but I think there are still three distinct patterns:

THE PAMPERERS

The first group is made up of people who, instead of getting their hurts doctored properly, pamper and favor it. These people, for whatever reason, have decided to hold on to that wound, even try to work around it. They might even honestly believe that they are required to suffer through life and even deserve this hurt they feel. Maybe they truly did something wrong in their past, so they think God is punishing them and they have to endure it—like a kind of penance.

But God doesn't want us harboring hurts and pain. Yes, we suffer consequences for our actions, but, should we repent of our actions, no matter how bad they are, it's God's desire that we be free and whole—not walking around through life wounded and defeated.

This group also includes the people who go around with their feelings on their sleeves. They carry that hurt openly for everyone to see, as if to say, "Hey, look. I've been hurt. Don't you feel sorry for me?" We've all met people who do this. These are the people, and don't you deny it, that we avoid at church functions if at all possible. And, for goodness's sake, if we do get near them, we don't dare ask them how they are. Every church has at least a couple of these dear people who truly believe that their pain should be worn like a badge of honor for the world to look at.

The sad thing, really, is that we've all been guilty of doing this at some point or another in our walk. I know I've personally enjoyed a pretty good pity party or two in my time. Haven't you? At some point, early on after my husband left, I must have realized that I needed to pick myself up, dust myself off, and get moving again. Not that I felt like it—I didn't. The hurt was a very real issue I had to deal with. I really felt that it must have been obvious to everyone around me that I was in severe pain, hurting beyond what words could even express, but then I noticed people at church coming up to me and saying things like, "I just found out what happened. I had no idea what you were going through. I never would have guessed it. You seem so strong!" I didn't know how to answer them. I didn't feel strong. How could they possibly think that?

There was only one explanation I could give. God's grace was poured out onto me in such a tremendous way in those months before and even after the divorce. The answer, quite simply, was that He'd given me a very close group of family and friends who knew the pain I was in, and their prayers began to cover me and the situation in which I found myself. That is the first thing our Lord will do for you, if you ask him. He even woke my friends and family up in the middle of the night with me on their hearts so that they could pray for me.

If you don't feel you have anyone to turn to, I suggest you contact your pastors for counseling and support in prayer—that's what they're there for. Pride will tell you not to burden them; one of the hardest phone calls I ever made during my time of hurt was to my pastor. It was the best thing I ever did, though—it connected me with someone who cared enough to pray for me and help me through it. I thank God every day for Pastor Hogan and his wife Brenda—I could never adequately express to them how much it meant to feel their support through prayer and some good, heartfelt counseling! Our choir director, James Polnick, also helped with his encouraging words during this time. A wonderful couple in our church spent time making themselves available to counsel my ex-husband and me through a very difficult time when we were trying to seek reconciliation. Sure, it didn't "take" with my ex-husband, but my point is that there are people who truly want to help if you just let them know you need it. God is capable of raising up an army to stand with us when war is raging.

If you aren't presently a member of any church, find one. Remember, no man is an island. If you're hurting and your heart is full of pain, let someone help you. (It helps if this person is a believer. If not, you might find that their advice won't be the same as what God wants you to hear.) Most of all, get in the Word of God. I believe that even a person who feels totally alone in his or her situation will gain peace in fellowship with Christ. He is that "friend that sticks closer than a brother" (Prov. 18:24). Unlike us humans, He'll never be in a hurry.

I know from experience that when you're in pain you might have difficulty praying for yourself. When we are so broken, sometimes we don't even know how to pray for ourselves—where do we begin? The pain is all we can see, if it is genuine pain. If you don't already have people praying for your situation, ask God to place your need on some strong Christian friends' hearts. God just has a special way of meeting us right where we are, if we ask Him to.

Please don't think that I'm suggesting that if you show any outward appearance of the pain you feel that you are wrong to do so; sometimes we cannot help but express our hurt, and most people who show their pain are not deliberately seeking attention. However, many people can either get so engrossed in the hurt that they'll forget that God can give them the peace that they need to survive in those hard times, or they simply won't be feeding themselves on God's Word.

God's Word is filled with passages that help us through hurtful times. In a minute, I'll share some of those with you, but first let's get back to the three ways I think people handle painful situations.

THE DENIERS

The second group denies they're hurting at all. Now, before you start thinking I'm nuts, just think about this for a minute. Remember in school how everyone laughed at the crybaby during recess? As a school teacher, believe me, I see this all the time. I have met many a child in school who've been told that it's a sign of weakness to admit that you're in pain or that you're hurt. Ever been at a sports game where somebody gets totally creamed? What's the first thing you hear either the coach or the fans saying? "Shake it off." But that's easy for others to say! They're not the one who got knocked flat by a gorilla!

We've been conditioned in our society to always look "tough." Some people have a very hard time admitting that they are hurting because they don't want to be different from everyone else. I've got some news for them: everybody hurts. Why wouldn't they want to admit that they're in real need of the first aid that only Jesus can give? Maybe they have a problem with pride; that is something that will keep the Lord from working in their lives. Or it could be that they've been fed large doses of teaching that says any admission of pain means that they don't have much faith, or that they must not be a very strong Christian.

Shocked? Well, you shouldn't be! I've been a Christian for fifty years, and I know there are well-meaning Christians out there—I'm sure I've been guilty of it myself—whose answer to another hurting brother or sister's problem has been, "Well, just have faith, and that situation will turn around. There's no need to fret. Just stand on His promises!" Not that the answer in itself is wrong. It's not. It's right on target. But before giving our usual memorized answer, think how we might make that person feel. Put yourself in the other person's shoes a minute. Here he or she is, with what might be a devastating personal injury. What that well-meaning Christian did with their flippant, almost casual response was make them feel that they don't have enough faith, or else they wouldn't be hurting.

I believe if this happens enough to a person, she will close herself off from getting help in the future. Eventually she may just decide, "Hey, I can deal with this myself. I'm OK. I don't need anyone else." She'll start denying that she's hurting, even to herself. However, closing herself off to other people could be the worst thing she could possibly do. By doing so, she's in danger of never getting the healing she so desperately needs.

Satan knows that with Christians, there is power in numbers. Remember Matthew 18:20: "Where two or three are gathered in my name, there I am in the midst of them." If Satan can deceive us into thinking we need to bear things alone and shut ourselves off from other Christians and hide the hurt, he's won a very important skirmish in this war against him.

I believe most people mean to be encouraging. They don't want to give a negative word, so the word they do speak comes out almost too casually. At this particular moment in life, though, people who are suffering need more than our words. They need us to put our arms around them, pray with them, and cry with them if necessary. They need us to be real with them.

THE ACCEPTORS

Last of all, we have what I consider to be the group with the best way to approach their painful circumstances. These are the people who recognize when they're hurting, and they do whatever the Lord wants them to do to receive His healing. They are not afraid of what others think. They're not ashamed to accept the peace and grace that the Lord freely offers to all who need them. They seek counseling and help from other believers, especially pastors or professional Christian counselors. And, most importantly, they fill their mind with His Word. Without it, no one can escape the hurts of this world. It doesn't hurt, either, to set your radio in your car and at home to the best Christian radio station you can find. This may seem like a small thing, but listening to praise and worship music will lift your spirits tremendously. These Christians have learned that we need to keep our mind on God in order to fight the battle of our emotions.

When my daughter told us that she was expecting a child at the young age of sixteen, I thought there could be nothing more painful to a mother's heart—until a good friend of mine lost her son to suicide.

When my husband walked out on me, I thought that nothing in a marriage could be more horrible—until I remembered that another teacher at my school had lost a year-long battle with cancer, leaving her family to continue life without her.

There is a wonderful woman at a church I attended once whose husband, shortly after their marriage, was in a terrible accident, leaving him almost totally paralyzed and unable to take care of himself, much less a new wife!

To be an acceptor, you have to let the Holy Spirit control your emotions. You need to realize that joy doesn't depend on your circumstances. It depends on a Savior who loves us and brings us through some terrible times only to bring us into a new, even more special relationship with Him. Your joy depends on our Lord God Almighty!

Jesus Christ shares in our sorrows. He lived on this earth and understands our pain because he was tempted in every way as we are now. He felt sadness, rejection, everything, just as we do. No wonder He has such a compassion for us when we are hurting! Who better to turn to when we're suffering the pains of this world?

I heard it said once that you have to look beyond what you see, even when your senses don't give you any assurances! When we are in the middle of hurtful circumstances, it's easy to just give up and give in to our emotions. To an extent, I believe we have to express those emotions, yes. But at some point, we need to give those emotions over to the Lord. We need to let Him pick those up, not "take on the world" by ourselves. Then we need to make a point to look past the hurts and focus on Him and on His promises.

Pastor Hogan has a saying he's quoted many times: "We've circled this mountain long enough. It's time to enter into the Promised Land!" This, of course, is in reference to the children of Israel who wandered around in the desert for forty years on a trip that should have taken only maybe a matter of weeks. The point is that if we don't lay our hurt feelings down at some point and move on, we may be just like them—we may be forfeiting a bright future that God has planned for us.

God doesn't intend for us to stay down. Psalm 34:19 says, "Many are the afflictions of the righteous, but the Lord delivers him from them all." He wants to deliver us from our pain, but we have to be willing to let Him do the healing work in us that is required.

Honestly, since we are all different individuals, and our experiences are and will continue to be very different, I cannot tell you how long it will take you to go through your season of sorrow or pain. Most of the time I feel I've made it through to the other side of this—and then something reminds me of my past life with my ex-husband and that old familiar pain returns. But now my sleep is peaceful, I don't cry over what I couldn't change, and I find myself actually enjoying my life and looking to the days ahead with a smile.

The Lord doesn't want it to be as hard as we make it! The trouble is that we're used to getting instant gratification to our needs in this society—people want answers like they get fast food. Most things—like divorce—don't just happen overnight, so why do some of us expect to get relief from our hurt and pain in an instant? We ask God to take it all away, and if it doesn't instantly disappear, we whine and complain that He apparently doesn't love us or isn't going to help us. But I think action is required on our part, not just God's.

First of all, take inventory. Ask God to show you what you need to do, yourself, to rise above the hurt you feel. Begin to stand on the promises in His Word. Honestly, you probably won't feel any different at first, but that's OK. If you encourage yourself daily and stay in daily communication with Him, as time goes by, you will begin to believe those promises for yourself; your emotions will catch up. The key in this is to remember that you absolutely cannot trust your emotions. If you are led by emotions only, you will find yourself on a roller coaster ride that you can't get off of! Trust Him. Trust His Word and what it says about you and your circumstances.

Some very powerful passages are in His Word to help us to get through hurtful times. Here are some words that I've found are extremely helpful. I know there are quite a few listed here, but when there is an aching, hurting heart, the strong medicine of His Word is necessary. I hope you let these really get into your heart, mind, and spirit.

> I would have lost heart, unless I had believed that I would see the goodness of the Lord in the land of the living.
> —Psa. 27:13

> The righteous cry out, and the Lord hears, and delivers them out of all their troubles. The Lord is near to those who have a broken heart, and saves such as have a contrite spirit. [This is one that I shared earlier, but it bears repeating!]
> —Psa. 34:17, 18

> You have hedged me behind and before, and laid your hand upon me. . . . Where can I go from Your Spirit? Or where can I flee from Your presence? If I ascend into heaven, You are there; if I make my bed in hell, behold You are there! [I find this particularly important to realize, because when we've been hurt we need to know He is right there with us. He sees our pain. He knows what we're going through!]
> —Psa. 139:5–8

> Arise, cry out in the night, at the beginning of the watches; pour out your heart like water before the face of the Lord. Lift up your hands toward Him.
> —Lam. 2:19a

You hold me by my right hand. You will guide me with Your counsel, and afterward receive me to glory. Whom have I in heaven but You? And there is none upon earth that I desire besides You. My flesh and my heart fail; but God is the strength of my heart and my portion forever.

—Psa. 73:23b–26

No temptation [or trial, troubles!] has overtaken you except such as is common to man; but God is faithful, who will not allow you to be tempted beyond what you are able, but with the temptation will also make the way of escape, that you may be able to bear it.

—1 Cor. 10:13

And let us not grow weary while doing good, for in due season we shall reap if we do not lose heart.

—Gal. 6:9

You number my wanderings, put my tears into Your bottle; are they not in Your book? When I cry out to You, then my enemies will turn back.

—Psa. 56:8, 9a

But you have seen, for You observe trouble and grief, to repay it by Your hand. The helpless commits himself to You. You are the helper of the fatherless.

—Psa. 10:14

You who have shown me great and severe troubles shall revive me again, and bring me up again from the depths of the earth. You shall increase my greatness and comfort me on every side.

— Psa. 71:20

[Paul, speaking of his "thorn in the flesh," says:] Concerning this I pleaded with the Lord three times that it might depart from me. [Don't we ask this of the Lord when we are hurting?] And He said to me, "My grace is sufficient for you, for My strength is made perfect in weakness."

—2 Cor. 12:8, 9a

We also glory in tribulations, knowing that tribulation produces perseverance; and perseverance, character; and character, hope. Now hope does not disappoint, because the love of God has been poured out in our hearts by the Holy Spirit who was given to us.

—Rom. 5:3b-5

You will not need to fight this battle. Position yourselves, stand still and see the salvation of the Lord, who is with you, oh Judah and Jerusalem! Do not fear or be dismayed [sorrowful, discouraged, hurt!]; tomorrow go out against them [the enemy], for the Lord is with you.

—2 Chron. 20:17

Unless the Lord had been my help, my soul would have settled in silence. If I say, "My foot slips," your mercy, O Lord, will hold me up.

—Psa. 94:17, 18

And the desire of the righteous will be granted. When the whirlwind passes by . . . the righteous have an everlasting foundation.

—Prov. 10:24b, 25

He also brought me up out of a terrible pit, out of a miry clay, and set my feet upon a rock, and established my steps. He has put a new song in my mouth—praise to our God... Blessed be the man who makes the Lord his trust and does not respect the proud, nor such as turn aside to lies.

—Psa. 40:2-4

THE HEALING OIL OF JOY

The Spirit of the Lord is upon me because the Lord has anointed Me to preach good tidings to the poor; He has sent Me to heal the brokenhearted, to proclaim liberty to the captives, and the opening of the prison to those who are bound; to proclaim the acceptable year of the Lord, and the day of vengeance to our God; to comfort all who mourn, to console those who mourn in Zion, to give them beauty for ashes [Hallelujah!], the oil of joy for mourning, the garment of praise for the spirit of heaviness [isn't that just what we're talking about?], that they may be called "trees of righteousness," the "planting of the Lord," that He may be glorified . . . and they shall rebuild the old ruins, they shall raise up the former desolations, and they shall repair the ruined cities, the desolations of many generations. [If you don't remember any of the other Scriptures listed here, get this one. It's incredible!]
—Isa. 61:1-4

Cast all your cares on Him, for He cares for you.
—1 Pet. 5:7

Set your mind on things above, not on earthly things.
—Col. 3:2

Chapter 6
SEEING THROUGH THE RAIN

> In the day of my trouble, I sought the Lord; my hand was stretched out in the night without ceasing; my soul refused to be comforted. I remembered God, and was troubled; I complained, and my spirit was overwhelmed.
>
> —Psa. 77:2, 3

You try to stand up, but immediately your ankle gives way. This is simply too much to bear. You're tired, hungry, and aware that if you can't walk, then you are in serious trouble. You can't just stay here. You must keep moving, but how? You can't put your weight on your foot, so how can you possibly move forward? You feel desperate for an answer to the pain and helplessness of it all.

You look for anything that might work as a crutch. Your ankle is beginning to swell, and you need to wrap it. You had the sense to pack some basic first aid supplies in your knapsack, so you pull them out and wrap your ankle. Now for something to hold you up.

To the side of a large pine, you find a limb that just might work as a crutch. You are aware of the irony that you aren't just stumbling physically through this forest. The fact that your whole life has become just as impossible to maneuver as this situation has not been lost on you. You're finding it hard to see a way out of this mess. Only now, when everything seems to be going wrong, do you finally realize that you can't fix your own life. You can't heal yourself. You can't make your compass work. You've tried. It hasn't worked so far and you know it never will. The things you've put your trust in to guide you through life have failed you. You need someone else to take over—someone who can heal the brokenness physically, but more importantly, emotionally. You can't keep going like you have been up until now, ignoring the pain and the need for help. It took getting lost and hurt to finally face the truth that you need God's help.

You let yourself cry, a release of all the control that you so doggedly wanted to hang onto. You allow yourself to let everything go and acknowledge that God knows what you need better than you do. "It's yours," you say aloud to the God who hears your heart. "Lead me."

For the first time in a long while, you sense that He is actually here, and you wait to see what He might be directing you to do. This is something new—this listening for direction instead of following your own instincts. You take your first step forward in faith.

I cannot address hurts, pains, regrets, or fear without touching on the topic of depression. In this life, when faced with all the "stuff" we deal with as humans, eventually we will all come face-to-face with some form of depression. For some, it may be a brief encounter, and then the darkness lifts. To others, it becomes a lifelong battle that cannot be overcome without some type of medical intervention. I am not one of the latter, thankfully. My encounters with depression have been short-lived but real enough that I know I don't want to go down that road if I can help it.

I remember the feelings well—or at least the results of the feelings. Wanting to shut out the world. Wanting to sleep, but even sleep drained my energy. Getting out of bed was asking too much. I didn't want to eat. Some days passed in a daze with little recollection of what I'd done all day.

I've known others who've been unfortunate enough to have lifelong battles with depression. My mother, though not clinically diagnosed or treated for it, suffered from depression. I believe that when my father left our family, she had an emotional breakdown. Even though outwardly most people might not have noticed, I'm almost positive that it threw her into a depression that lasted for several years. Other family members have had their bouts with it as well. I know my ex-husband faced it over twenty years ago, as well as during the last few years of our marriage.

My daughter most definitely battled it during the months of her pregnancy. There were many days that I hated leaving her alone to go to work, because quite honestly I wasn't sure of her state of mind. I called her many times throughout the day to check on her to make sure she was OK.

We tend to shut others out when we're depressed. One sign that experts tell you to look for, especially with teenage depression, is whether the person is shutting him or herself in behind the closed door of their room every day (especially if they are usually a very social person).

Depression is a dark, debilitating enemy. I know that there are people who have chemical imbalances in the brain that cause depression, and it can be treated as any other type of disease with medication and therapy. I know that others are only thrown into it because of situations that come into their lives.

This is, in my opinion, one of the most misunderstood maladies known to man. Because it is misunderstood, often it is also swept under the rug, especially in Christian circles, and not talked about as it probably should be. Because of that, many suffer from it silently, not wanting fellow Christians to know about it. I think that's a terrible testimony to us in the Christian walk. The Bible tells us to "bear one another's burden," but this is a burden that often goes unspoken. People don't want to admit that they have this problem. Whether this is pride, embarrassment, or fear of judgment from other Christians, we all need to practice grace with ourselves and with others.

Depression causes you to lose your vision for life. My daughter told me that at least when she was sleeping, she "didn't have to think." Waking up means facing reality, and reality is, well, too real. Waking up means facing the pain, uncertainty, fear, and even the unexpected torments.

Once, I was shopping with my daughter at a shoe store. We weren't in there long before they started playing a beautiful love song that just happened to be one that was played at our wedding. Well, guess what? I not only lost the joy of shopping for shoes, I spent the next two days of my weekend crying in between everyday household chores, wondering if it would ever be possible to free myself of the pain.

While that song played in the store, many happy moments spent with my young groom way back in 1976 played in my head. The loving looks that he'd saved only for me. His tender touch. The words he once whispered in my ear. I couldn't have stopped it from flooding my brain if I'd been furnished with my very own remote control.

There was a popular song recorded back in the '70s by the Bee Gees that sums up the emotions I was feeling. It shares the feelings of a man, who in his youth only thought about living his life with no possibility of sorrow touching him. Yet years later, having gone through the pain and sorrow of a broken heart, he now wonders how life could go on as if nothing had ever happened. The sun still shines, the rain falls and the world is still spinning as usual. He questions how he will ever be whole again. He's asking for help in the midst of his pain. He just wants to live again.

I honestly can't count the number of times in the last fourteen years that I've completely understood the dilemma of this songwriter. Depression leaves us empty, sad, alone. The darkness settles in. How does everyone else in the world appear to just go on as if it were of no significance? It feels as though the sun shouldn't shine and the stars shouldn't twinkle. But they do. Then we are faced with the realization that we're the ones out of sync with the rest of the world, and the depression only worsens.

The truth is that other people are hurting as well, but we can't see them, because all we see is what our own narrow vision allows us to see. In times of extreme hurt or depression, our vision is limited. *Our* pain, *our* hurt, *our* loss become our only focus. If we can grasp that fact, we stand a chance at fighting back at this enemy of depression. And who, my friend, is the one who brings the cloud of depression into so many of our lives? Satan, of course, is our enemy. You see, if he can get us focused on ourselves and on our problems, then he can deceive us into thinking that we have no future and that we won't do anything else with this life God blessed us with. There's nothing he'd like better than to convince a believer that all hope is gone, that our future is a brick wall, that we'll never rise above the depression that has settled over us.

Once, I was thrown into another short bout of depression that made me physically ill. It started over a situation at Christmastime.

The previous year, my son had married the most beautiful, loving little girl a mother-in-law could ask for. Ben and Ashley are perfect for each other; both seem to naturally complete the other. It is one thing (not the only thing, mind you) that has brought me so much joy in these past years, despite what happened in my own marriage.

However, I decided that I would let my wishes be known to my son this particular Christmas: I wanted them to have Christmas Eve at my house, since they'd been other places the past couple of years. I felt I was "due," I guess. It was my "right" as his mom, right? Well, not only was the thought wrong, but the way I handled it was as well. I called my son's cell phone, and, not getting ahold of him, I left a message. I don't know about you, but I do better with a live person on the other end of the line. Somehow in that brief message I didn't just ask for them to come over. I conveyed a feeling (not meaning to) that my daughter-in-law was a control freak and was making my son go to all her relatives' houses, forgetting about me.

Don't ask how I managed to do that—I'm not sure, myself—but it was the farthest thing from my mind. I simply wanted to spend time with both of my kids, my daughter-in-law, and grandson on this particular Christmas Eve. But, somehow, in my ramblings with his voicemail, I succeeded in saying everything wrong.

When I did hear from my son, I could tell from his voice that something was amiss. He let me know my message had upset him and Ashley, and that she was not a control freak. I tried my best to apologize, for hurting Ashley was not my intent. The words "control freak" had never even been spoken. However, whatever I had said, the damage had been done. He, reacting to what he thought was an accusation on my part, went on to tell me that it was his choice to be with her family on Christmas Eve. It's where he wanted to be. When he explained why, I interpreted him to mean that there would be more people at Ashley's family celebration, more fun, and that was that.

I realized, later, that his intent was not to make me feel unworthy of their presence on Christmas Eve. He was just responding to what he thought were my accusations. Later, I called and apologized personally to my daughter-in-law, as I needed to. But for hours before that, I sobbed. I had been jolted once again into remembering that everything in my life had changed. My husband was gone. My son, in my mind, had just told me he didn't want to be at our house where we'd all spent so many Christmases together. It would, once again, be just me, my daughter, and our grandson.

Do you hear what I'm saying? I was having a pity party, and I still had so much to be thankful for! Instead of focusing on what I still had, I chose to dwell on what I felt I'd lost. And, in reality, I hadn't even lost it. I still have my son's and daughter-in-law's love. But for hours I had convinced myself that I'd lost them too. How do we manage to get so messed up in our thinking?

I was totally consumed with thoughts of myself—how I'd been misunderstood. I was, once again, being unappreciated by someone close to me. A conversation with my daughter that afternoon started me back on the right path. Before she got off the phone, she said something that gave me a reality check. I had said, "I can't help it that your dad left! Nothing will ever be the same again!" I was assuming that if Ben didn't enjoy being there, it must be because his dad was no longer there.

She responded, "Mom, forget all of that. We both still have Jordan. Isn't that important?"

You bet it is.

It's true that things will never be the same again. But, realistically, would I really want them to be? Of course not. One thing I've learned for sure is that if things always stay the same, we aren't making progress. Whether I liked it or not, things changed in my life. So I picked myself up and went to the bathroom to blow my nose and dry my tears. I put my makeup back on, and sat down, and picked up the book I'd just bought for myself. I began to take note mentally of all the blessings (like Jordan, my only grandchild at that time) that were mine.

What had taken place that day had really been an example of the spiritual battles that we, as Christians, go through so often. This is important to note, for if the enemy can get us to a place where we feel defeated, depression will follow close behind. We fight most of our battles in our own mind. If we take a beating there, we've lost big time.

The enemy of our souls knows where we are the most vulnerable, maybe even better than we ourselves know. For example, I am aware, as he is, that one of my weak spots in the past has been in the area of self-esteem. Whether it's because of my divorce, or as I have since figured out, from something further back in my history—my father abandoning my mother and siblings and me when I was eight years old. I've often struggled with feelings of inadequacy.

The good news here is that throughout this healing process I'm in, the Lord has revealed a lot about me—to me. You see, God knows us too. He's shown me that I need to lay my feelings down at the altar of my heart and give them over to Him, totally. For a while on this day, those hidden insecurities had surfaced, and Satan, for a while, had had me convinced that I'd failed miserably at being a mother, just as I had thought I'd failed at being a wife. I think that there are times when God allows us to face setbacks like this so He can help us to see those broken areas in our hearts that need healing. Instead of fighting against the process, we need to ask Him why we react to things the way we do, and when did those things first affect us, so that He can shed His light on the situation and bring ultimate healing.

You see, Satan can't do anything we don't let him do. We are so much more powerful in Christ than we even realize. God has so much for us and works on our behalf all of the time. All Satan can do is to trick us into wrong thinking, which will lead us away from the joyful, victorious life that God has planned for us. I don't know about you, but I'm pretty sick and tired of him.

A lot of our problems stem from a lack of belief. Yes, we may be Christians. Yes, we know what the Word says about life and how He wants us to live it. Yes, we pray both for ourselves and others. But in reality, when it gets right down to the nitty-gritty of life, where's our faith? Doesn't He have every answer right there, readily available for us at every turn, if we'd just have the faith to step out and believe for it? So many of us fail to believe for our own selves what we have no trouble believing for someone else.

Depression has so many people in its grip that thousands of people commit suicide on a daily basis. Teenage suicide is running rampant. Desperation in a world of chaos is the reality we face in America and around the globe. Never before has there been such a need for answers to a growing population of hurting people.

Personally, I believe that's because time as we know it is growing very short. The enemy knows how limited his time is, and if he can't defeat us one way, then he'll try his best to defeat us in another way. His favorite playground is our minds. He knows how powerful we can be if we exercise our faith in a mighty God the way that the Lord intended. So Satan works his deceptive mind-control game wherever we allow him to. He starts by making us think we're defeated when we're really not. It's our limited vision of who we are (and most importantly, who God is) that defeats us! God is a big God. He can do all things. But, just as in those examples in the Bible of people Jesus healed, He sometimes asks us, "Do You believe I can do this?" Didn't he also say many times, "According to the faith that is in you, be healed"? The key is not in whether or not God can heal us. The key is, do we truly believe that He can?

I don't for a moment pretend that I have all the answers for everybody. But He does. I may not know all of your circumstances, just as you don't know everything that I've faced. But He knows us all completely. He knows every hurt. He's seen every tear. As His word says in Psalm 56:8, "You number my wanderings, put my tears into Your bottle; are they not in Your book?" Jesus not only knows about it—He's felt the same hurts. There's nothing we've felt that He hasn't. He came to earth to become a man, was tempted in every way as we are, rejected, persecuted, bruised, beaten, spat upon, tortured and crucified. That's why He is the only One who is able to make intercession for us daily to the Father for our needs. Who better to heal us from depression than Jesus Christ?

If you're in the heat of the battle in the area of depression, ask God to give you back your vision. Be totally honest and let Him hear from you about how you're feeling right now. As you pour out your heart before Him, make a decision to listen to what He, alone, says about who you are. Ask Him to help you place your eyes back on Him instead of focusing your eyes on yourself and the problems you're facing right now. Remember, the bigger you make your problems, the smaller He becomes! Begin to believe He is able to do everything that His Word promises He can do. The key word here is BELIEVE!

God has given us a wonderful gift in the Holy Spirit. If you are a believer, His Spirit is with you every day to help you. Together, God the Father, the Son, and the Holy Spirit—in agreement with you, in prayer—make a powerful team that the enemy can't stand against. Remember, Satan is more afraid of you than you realize. That's why he's fighting to deceive you in your mind: so he'll be able to gain ground. Don't even give him an inch.

May these Scriptures minister to you today, and help you to see that He alone can raise you up and help you through whatever degree of depression you feel. Seek Him for the help you need. Get some Godly counselor to walk with you until you're strong enough to face things yourself. Don't be afraid to talk about your depression to others. I think you'll find there are others who are facing similar situations, and He'll lead you to people who will be there to lift you up in prayer when you feel the walls closing in on you.

> Why are you cast down, O my soul? And why are you disquieted within me? Hope in God, for I shall yet praise Him for the help of His countenance. . . .The Lord will command His loving-kindness in the daytime, and in the night, His song shall be with me—a prayer to the God of my life.
> —Psa. 42:5-8

> When you pass through the waters, I will be with you; and through the rivers, they shall not overflow you. When you walk through the fire, you shall not burned, nor shall the flame scorch you, for I am the Lord your God . . . and I have loved you . . . Fear not, for I am with you.
> —Isa. 43:2-5a

> "For your Maker is your husband, The Lord of hosts is His name; and your Redeemer is the Holy One of Israel; He is called the God of the whole earth. For the Lord has called you like a woman forsaken and grieved in spirit. . .For a mere moment I have forsaken you, but with great mercies I will gather you. . .For the mountains shall depart and

the hills be removed, but My kindness shall not depart from you, nor shall my covenant of peace be removed," says the Lord who has mercy on you.

—Isa. 54:5-7, 10

For now we see in a mirror, dimly, but then [when we see Christ] face to face. Now I know in part [I don't see the whole picture!], but then I shall know just as I also am known. And now abide faith, hope, love, these three.

—1 Cor. 13:12, 13a

For we do not know what we should pray for as we ought, but the Spirit Himself makes intercession for us with groanings which cannot be uttered. Now He who searches the hearts knows what the mind of the Spirit is, because He makes intercession for the saints according to the will of God. And we know that all things work together for good to those who love God, to those who are the called according to His purpose.

—Rom. 8:26b-28

Therefore, having been justified by faith, we have peace with God through our Lord Jesus Christ, through whom also we have access by faith into this grace in which we stand, and rejoice in hope of the glory of God. And not only that, but we also glory in tribulations, knowing that tribulation produces perseverance; and perseverance, character; and character, hope.

—Rom. 5:1-4

I will both lie down in peace, and sleep [How many times have we suffered sleepless nights due to depression, grieving?]; For You alone, O Lord, make me dwell in safety.

—Psa. 4:8

Blessed is the man whom You instruct, O Lord, and teach out of Your law, that you may give him rest from the days of adversity, until the pit is dug for the wicked. For the Lord will not cast off His people, nor will He forsake His inheritance.

—Psa. 94:12-14

I will lift up my eyes to the hills—from whence comes my help? My help comes from the Lord, who made heaven and earth.

—Psa. 121:1, 2

Chapter 7

ISLANDS CAN BE LONELY

A man's pride will bring him low, but the humble in spirit will retain honor.

—Prov. 29:23

You can see the sun straight up above and know which direction to go for now. But parts of the forest are so dense that you can get turned around easily. Not having your compass is definitely a disadvantage, but now that you've asked God to lead you, you can feel yourself wanting to test your faith and believe in His direction. It feels unnatural, yet right. You're out of practice with trusting God. Can you really let go of the controls of the situation and trust God to bring you out of this? You've always been too proud to let someone else tell you what to do before. When facing problems, you always lead with, "I can do this," or "I know what to do. There's nothing I can't tackle. I'll figure this out." This bowing to God's wisdom and authority and letting Him lead you feels strange, yet somehow it's just what you need to do. After all, look where your pride has gotten you so far—it hasn't served you too well, has it? Maybe it's OK to admit you don't know everything!

You strongly sense that something is urging you in the direction of a small clearing to the left, a certainty that you haven't felt for the last two days. You know it's God. If you could just find your campsite, you'd be closer to getting to your car, parked up off of the main highway just a few miles away. As you trek on, you continue to *pray for guidance. You feel the battle raging within you: do you allow your pride to rule, only trusting your own instincts, or do you release it and accept the guidance you're beginning to sense from God?*

You're so deep in prayer, with your eyes focused on the path in front of you, that you haven't looked up for several moments. When you finally do, your breath catches. In front of you is a small building to the right of the path, not twenty yards ahead. You might not have found the path out of here, but He's led you to something even better for the moment—something that represents civilization. A cabin.

~ ~ ~ ~

I heard it said somewhere that one of the most common reasons that marriages fail is a lack of communication. Others say that it is selfishness that causes the most trouble in relationships. Probably if you listened to all the experts on the subject, they would all point fingers at these and other culprits such as lying (lack of honesty), finances, the stress of jobs (especially in these modern times when both spouses usually have careers), and the stress of raising a family. The list of reasons is probably endless.

I've often found myself contemplating just exactly where everything derailed in my life, specifically in my marriage. I've already said before, there's really no need to waste energy trying to figure out something that cannot be "fixed"—but, at the risk of stirring things up a bit, let me say that, personally, I think pride took a front-row seat in my circumstances.

Pride is probably the hardest culprit to see in ourselves, but somehow we can always see it in everybody else! Pride, unlike anger or fear, doesn't have a definite form. It's ever-so-subtle and can mask itself better than any other enemy of our Christian walk. Anger is usually loud, and you can't miss the sting it leaves behind—not to mention an elevation in blood pressure. Fear is a pretty obvious enemy too, unless we're knee-deep in denial.

Pride, though, can come across as anything from outright arrogance in some people, to seemingly harmless forms associated with those not wanting to "burden" others with their troubles or "air their dirty laundry," leading them not to ask for help in situations when they might genuinely need it. This person is often just considered a "private" person who doesn't want to "make a fuss"—when in actuality, they may not want anyone to know that they are having problems.

Even someone with low self-esteem can be exercising a form of pride. The first time I heard someone say that, I was taken aback, but it makes sense. If we are constantly comparing ourselves to others, never seeing ourselves as "measuring up," then we are too focused on "me." All focus and energy is spent on *me*, making *me* look better, so that *my* needs then become more important than those of anyone close to me. Isn't that part of what pride does? It overemphasizes who we think we are.

Looking back, it was so easy for me to see how my ex-husband had a problem with pride. And truly, I did (and still do for that matter) see where pride came into the picture. It was there every time he didn't talk about things that might've been bothering him, which happened more and more frequently as the years passed. It was there when my daughter had a child at such a young age, and he hated what people were thinking and saying about her, about him as her father, about all of us. He was sure everyone would think he'd failed as a father. Suddenly, he felt all eyes were on us as a family. He never liked being put in any spotlight, under the scrutiny of others.

But after all the months of scrutinizing every word, spoken or unspoken, between us, I finally realized something. While I was spending so much time pointing a finger at what pride was doing, and had done, in his life, I failed to take a look at my own motives for things I'd done. Sadly, the real truth is that we're all guilty of exhibiting pride. No one wants to admit it—probably because we're too proud.

It was pride that kept me from calling my husband right after he left. He'd hurt me. Blindsided me. I never even saw it coming. I wanted him to come back and admit that he was wrong and apologize. If my pride had taken a back seat, if I'd just picked up the phone, maybe we could've mended things before he travelled too far down that road leading him away from me. There's no way to know if we actually could, but the possibility is there. What stopped me? I couldn't bear the thought that he'd reject me again. My pride wouldn't allow me to find out.

I see now how pride can come in and knock us flat in our walk. First Corinthians 10:12 comes to mind: "Therefore, let him who thinks he stands take heed, lest he fall." How true that is. Every day we need to pray, "Lord, keep me from being proud!" It is so subtle that we don't even recognize it, even when we're in the grip of it—*especially* when we're in the grip of it.

Pride has a way of biting back, too. Many years ago, a young teenage girl we both knew became pregnant. I still can remember telling my husband, "Well, all I know is that no daughter of mine is going to act like that! Where were her parents in all of this? Couldn't they control their own daughter?"

Oh what I'd give to take those words back! Only a few years later I faced the same heartbreaking situation with our own daughter, and immediately, the other girl came to my mind.

Of course, God came through in our darkest hour. I know firsthand that the Lord can turn what the enemy intends for hurt and devastation into something incredibly beautiful—I can't imagine our lives without my grandson. What a gift he has been. Of course, there are consequences for any sin, but we can rise above the heartache if we give God the controls!

If we knock pride down once, chances are we're going to have to keep knocking it down. By now, I'm sure you've noticed, pride presents itself to us daily. To some people, it happens more than we can count.

My ex-husband and I had very different temperaments, so we responded to situations in very different ways. One night, after an incident involving a boy our daughter was dating, my then-husband lost his temper. I attempted to talk to him about it, but I only managed to make things worse. He was angry—more than I'd ever seen him before. I was a bit scared. When I went in to talk to my daughter later, she asked me what I thought at the time to be the most ridiculous question she could ever have asked me: "Are you and Dad going to divorce?"

"What?" I remember asking, incredulously. "Of course not. Your dad and I may have disagreements, but for heaven's sake, why would you ask me that?" However, she continued to voice her concern that her dad would leave me.

I told her we'd been together for more than twenty-five years, and her dad would never do something like that. It might happen to other people, but it would not happen in this family. He wasn't that kind of person. We weren't that way. We'd never quit.

Satan must love pride over any other kind of sin in a Christian's walk, because pride breeds all kinds of other sins once it starts. It can topple your life, toppling bit-by-bit, like a long line of dominoes.

Within two months of that conversation with my daughter, my husband left. He told me later that he never would've believed that he was capable of doing all that he did in that first year after the divorce. He surprised even himself. Why? Because he proudly thought it wasn't possible—that he couldn't ever do those things. Our marriage was too strong. It was impossible. It couldn't be done. But it happened.

No, what happened was the result of pride, along with anger and bitterness coming in and knocking down intimacy, companionship, loyalty, trust, friendship and all of the other good things that our marriage had consisted of for so long. You've heard the expression, "It just takes one bad apple to spoil the basket"? Pride is the bad "apple" we need to be sure to keep out of our marriages, relationships, and lives.

I can speak about this as one who knows because the enemy has tried to use it to "topple" my world in more than one area of my life. It managed to destroy my marriage. It tried to bring down my relationship with my daughter after her father left. She and I now have a very positive relationship, but we wouldn't have gotten there without some tough lessons that the Lord taught me while I was on my knees. And pride will, no doubt, continue to threaten every relationship I'm in for the rest of my life.

God wants us to get rid of everything that hinders our Christian walk, and I've not seen too many things that can hinder it as much as pride. I've reached the point in my life that I want more of Him than I've ever had before, but He will require me to eliminate this issue of pride.

There are two dominant problems found in our flesh: pride and selfishness. These two go hand in hand, for where pride is present, selfishness isn't far behind. If we could only get these two problems under control in our lives, God could do things we never could imagine. Pride cannot handle criticism; it tries to impress people; it gets embarrassed. Pride is opinionated, always has the last word, and is quick to judge. When you add selfishness to it, we are no longer able to love the people around us properly.

It is humility that causes God to promote us. Humility is a "force" of the heart—simply walking in the reality of God's Word. It's knowing who we are in Him and following His example. Then we can see others not as a threat, or even as people we have to impress. We simply begin to serve them instead of looking to them to serve us and meet our needs.

The key is to pray that the Lord help us to be more like Him in this area. Jesus came to this world in an unimpressive stable and was raised by a carpenter. He came not as people thought the King of the Jews would come, but as a man of humility with a servant's heart, showing mercy and grace to anyone who needed it. He wasn't loud or demanding of people, quick to judge or to put people down. He never lashed out when he didn't get his way or judge Himself better than the rest of humanity. Instead He became as one of us, though He was the Son of God!

Here are just a few of the Scriptures that deal with pride:

By pride comes nothing but strife, but with the well-advised is wisdom.
—Prov. 13:10

The Pharisee stood and prayed thus with himself, "God, I thank you that I am not like other men—extortionists, unjust, adulterers, or even as tax collectors. I fast twice a week; I give tithes of all that I possess."

And the tax collector, standing afar off, would not so much as raise his eyes to heaven, but beat his breast, saying, "God, be merciful to me a sinner!" I tell you, this man went down to his house justified rather than the other; for everyone who exalts himself will be humbled, and he who humbles himself will be exalted.
—Luke 18:11-14

Therefore, let him who thinks he stands take heed, lest he fall.
—1 Cor. 10:12

Though the Lord is on high, yet He regards the lowly; but the proud He knows from afar.
—Psa. 138:6

A man's pride will bring him low, but the humble in spirit will retain honor.
—Prov. 29:23

May the Lord cut off all flattering lips, and the tongue that speaks proud things, who have said, "With our tongue we will prevail; Our lips are our own; Who is lord over us?"
—Psa. 12:3, 4

For You will save the humble people, but will bring down haughty looks.

—Psa. 18:27

For if anyone thinks himself to be something, when he is nothing, he deceives himself.

—Gal. 6:3

For who makes you differ from another? And what do you have that you did not receive? Now if you did indeed receive it, why do you boast as if you had not received it?

—1 Cor. 4:7

Pride goes before destruction, and a haughty spirit before a fall. Better to be of a humble spirit with the lowly, than to divide the spoil with the proud.

—Prov. 16:18, 19

PART THREE
INCREASED VISIBILITY

Chapter 8

OUT OF FOCUS

Being confident of this very thing, that He who has begun a good work in you will complete it until the day of Jesus Christ.

—Philip. 1:6

Shelter! It was a long afternoon hobbling down this path on a poor excuse for a crutch. The thought of staying inside a building tonight (that is, if you can get in) instead of out in the open makes you feel as if you're entering a luxury hotel instead of the little shed in front of you. The need to feel safe and secure is overwhelming. You feel insecure, not just unprotected from the elements, but unsure of yourself and your ability to do what's required to survive out here. Do you really have what it takes to get yourself out of this mess? That's a new one! Lack of confidence was never a problem before. Or was it? What a strange moment to realize that a lot of the tough persona you exude in front of people might just be a mask to conceal how unsure you really feel inside. Has anyone believed the lie that you have confidence when you're really just pretending? You shake off the thought as you reach for the door. Time to act, not daydream!

The door seems locked at first, but when you give it a hard shove, it gives way to an abandoned cabin—one too small for anyone to actually live there. It doesn't have any furniture in it except for a small wooden chair in the far corner. Was this a place a park ranger used when he or she was in this part of the woods? Did this land actually belong to someone?

A quick search for food reveals nothing. Your snacks are running low, so you'll have to make them stretch, but for how long? It is already Sunday evening. You're beginning to feel shaky from hunger. You've been walking around these woods for two whole days now without running into anyone or finding your way back to camp. How many more days would you have to go before being found? You can't shake off the helpless feelings again, though you're grateful for a place to stay. Finding the cabin seems only to magnify your awareness of how lost you still are—you still have no idea how far you have to go to get back to your car. You try to ignore the hunger pangs, and look for what else you could find in the cabin that might help you through another night.

That's when you notice a bookshelf. It doesn't have many books on it, but it is holding a picture of a man, a woman, and a teenage girl. The person who owns this cabin must have a family, and that knowledge comforts you. Surely a family man won't mind your trespassing.

~ ~ ~ ~

We all long for companionship. Most of us women seek the security of having someone to hold us, take care of us, make us feel safe. The desire to have someone to love and to receive love from is something that was placed in every woman by God Himself. He made us this way. It's part of who we are. While men want a sense of accomplishment and feeling appreciated for what they do, women are driven, often, by a need for security.

When that security is no longer there, it makes for some very scary feelings. I've shared most of those already, and I think I've come pretty far in resolving (with God's help) those feelings of fear, anger, hurt, resentment, and even depression. I guess the one lingering battle that still remains to be conquered is the one I have with my own feelings of insecurity at times. Between having a father who deserted the family when I was only eight and being abandoned by a husband of twenty-five—almost twenty-six—years, I've received many suggestions from the enemy that there must be something wrong with me. Otherwise, I wouldn't be sitting here alone. He is, of course, a liar. But his voice is the one that demands attention at times.

Other women seem to have it all, right? They have husbands who shower them with attention, support, adoration, and, most importantly, their time. They are there when they need them. They listen to them. They make them feel special.

Never am I more aware of what I'm missing than when I spend time with my daughter-in-law's parents—those two have such a great relationship. You know their love goes deep. You sense their support for each other. When one needs something, the other is quick to respond. It's not that their marriage is perfect or that they haven't faced their share of adversity, but they've learned how to make it work despite whatever else might be going on. Jamie and Joel Perkins have four grown daughters, six grandchildren, a thriving restaurant business, and active roles in their community. They entertain people in their home; yet somehow, in this very busy life they have, they have managed to maintain a good, healthy relationship in their marriage. It may be presumptuous of me, since I'm only surmising this in what I've observed, but I think I'm safe in saying that these two know how to make it work. I have to admit that over the course of the last fourteen years since I've met these great people, I've had to push down feelings of—yes, I'll admit it—envy. Many times, especially at the wedding of our two children shortly after my divorce, when I struggled to keep the tears back in the face of my ex-husband, I looked at these two with some good old-fashioned jealousy. I definitely had to pray about my attitude and give it to the Lord.

I wanted what they had. I felt cheated, robbed. It wasn't fair. So, as he so often does, Satan shoved it in my face. I assumed I must not have been "good enough" to have what they have. I must not have had what it takes to keep a man by my side. My man, my dreams for the future, my very life, had been taken from me by someone else who was now living my life. I guessed she (the other woman) must have had something I didn't have. What was I lacking?

Deep down, I know the lies for what they were, but sometimes, especially at emotional occasions like the wedding of my son, instead of enjoying the festivities, all my insecurities come to the surface. At an event where most people had come in couples, I felt painfully, obviously alone. It didn't matter that my former husband was sitting beside me—I was alone. I felt as if I had a sign on my chest reading, in big print, "LOSER!" If you have never been in that position yourself, then let me congratulate you for being one of the very few totally secure people walking on the planet. Whatever made you so secure you ought to bottle it and patent it, because most of us have at least one area, if we're honest enough to admit it, where we feel we are lacking in some way.

Most of the time, I feel fairly confident, but put me in a room filled with nothing but married people, and I'll start feeling inadequate—wrongly so, mind you, but there you are!

I'm not a stranger to feelings of insecurity. When I was only six or seven years old, I had a bout with rheumatic fever. I imagine I must have been ill for quite some time before my parents knew what was wrong with me. With four children ranging from six to fourteen at the time and very little income (my dad worked in a bakery, and Mom stayed home to take care of us), doctor visits were rare. They couldn't afford to take us to the doctor for every little ache and pain. My aches and pains, however, became more and more severe. I would run a fever, have a sore throat, then suffer from leg cramps that I still remember as excruciating. We didn't know then what we do now about strep, and how important it is to be treated with antibiotics to rid the body of the infection. Strep had led to rheumatic fever, which we know now attacks different organs of the body if untreated—in my case specifically, the heart. By the time they did take me to the doctor, I'd developed a heart murmur as well.

To make a long story short, God eventually performed a miracle. He healed me of the rheumatic fever and the heart murmur as well. However, I'd missed most of the second grade. I had spent day after day lying around, unable to go outside and play with friends. (Because of this, I eventually had no friends.) My mom had been told that I needed to rest, and even after my healing she continued to be extremely protective of me. I guess at my young age I didn't realize just how sick I was—I just knew how bad I felt.

When I was allowed to go back to school, I wasn't allowed to participate in anything too physical, which made me the oddball of the class. I became introverted and painfully self-conscious. The few kids I did reach out to were never the ones who were "popular." I perceived myself as being not good enough—different, somehow, from everyone else.

Then, of course, my parents' divorce compounded the feelings of inferiority. We weren't exactly the Cleavers—*they* never got a divorce. Nor did Rob and Laura Petrie or any other idolized family that we watched each night on the television screen. We, unfortunately, were a "modern" family—out-of-place in a naïve Eisenhower/Kennedy/"Camelot" era. Not that we wanted to be, or even asked to be that kind of family. Mom, I'm sure, didn't want to deal with a shattered marriage. Her children didn't ask to be uprooted and moved to another city in order to escape the fallout of the breakup. But, there we were, broken and hurting.

As I grew up, I never thought of myself as a natural beauty, but I never minded terribly. Oh, I was OK to look at, but as I hit adolescence, I was taller than most girls my age, and my long legs seemed to do nothing but get in the way. My "awkward" stage seemed to last forever. I watched with envy my classmates join in team sports and appear to blossom, as I tried desperately to just "fit in."

High school was not the most enjoyable time of my life, either. All these feelings of inadequacy came to the surface. While everyone else seemed to be dating, I convinced myself that I was content to just be everyone's buddy or little sister. I considered the one "boyfriend" I had during high school to be more of a friend. We only went on a handful of dates. The truth was that I didn't have the confidence in myself to even talk to the opposite sex—especially someone I was attracted to.

Looking back on it, I probably was better off that way, but at the time it was difficult because I believed I was somehow different. I hid behind jokes and my sense of humor to get me through awkward moments when I was trapped and had to talk to someone. I figured if I made it a joke, I'd at least look like I was confident! I had most people fooled, but deep down, I was a very insecure person.

In my devotional once I read a quote from Charlie Brown: "It goes back to when I first set foot on the stage of my life. They looked at me and said, 'He's just not right for the part!'" That was how I felt most of my early life. I just didn't think I was right for the part.

Unfortunately these feelings of poor self-image carried over into my young adult life as well. They even spilled over into my marriage. They usually surfaced in small ways, like my habit of speaking negatively (usually about myself) to other people—even my husband. God has brought me far in this, and I usually recognize it for what it is now—there has been much inner healing taking place in the last few years especially—but Satan also knows our weak points and will continue to come back and try to trip us up in those areas, whatever they may be. It will be that way until Jesus comes.

Of course, I hadn't learned the truth about Satan's lies yet back all those years ago; I was definitely listening to the wrong voice about who I was. Our self-image, it has been said, is second only to our faith in God—but it's hard to have faith in God and believe the good things God says about you when you can't see them yourself. Not only does a wrong self-image defeat us, but it also affects our relationships with other people. It's hard to love people around you properly when you don't love yourself.

What I'm talking about here is a spiritual stronghold. A stronghold is anything that holds us back from a closer walk with the Lord. It keeps us from moving deeper with Him and becoming all that He wants us to become. It holds us back because whatever it might be it directs our focus off of God and onto it. Some examples are the strongholds of suspicion, doubt, fear, confusion, independence (usually because we've been hurt by someone), pride, or low self-esteem. The list is probably endless. Some people might call these "hang-ups." Whatever we call them, God wants to free us of them.

In my case, this low self-image kept me from probably a hundred things that God intended for me to do in my life. The losses I've faced, along with words spoken over me as a child (and even as I grew), caused me to have a false image of myself. I've always had a desire to be used by the Lord in whatever way He intends, but how many times have I stepped back, fearful that I just didn't have what it would take? "Surely," I would think to myself, "I'm just not qualified," or "I don't have the talent," or "Someone else would probably do a better job." These are just a few of my former go-to excuses for not stepping out in faith and doing what I believe God desired me to do.

There is a Scripture that says that a person should "not think of himself more highly than he ought to think, but to think soberly, as God has dealt to each one a measure of faith," (Rom. 12:3). Let's get some balance here, though. This verse tells us that we need to be careful not to become puffed up or arrogant people who are all about themselves—and goes on to talk about us all being members of one body. We all need each other. I believe many of us don't hold any esteem for ourselves at all. How this must hurt God's heart. He was the one who created us. By thinking so poorly of ourselves, aren't we thinking poorly of Him as our Creator? He was the one who formed us in our mother's womb just as we are. As we grow up, we all face our own unique set of circumstances that help to mold and change us as we mature into adults. These circumstances are where the enemy begins to hurl those fiery darts at us, making us doubt ourselves and God.

I looked up the word *esteem* in the dictionary recently. One of the definitions of esteem is "to regard as valuable." Why is it that some of us are so averse to this idea of regarding ourselves as valuable? I'm including myself in this group, believe me, because for at least most of my younger life I considered it almost a sin if I said or thought any good thing about myself. This became a kind of false humility, really. Humility is *not* the same as self-deprecation. To be humble doesn't mean undervaluing or belittling ourselves. Guess what I found out? It's OK to love myself! God actually wants me to regard myself as valuable because I am valuable to Him. Therein lies the victory over my insecurities and yours.

But because someone else failed to make me feel loved, cherished, accepted, or valuable to them, I felt I had no value—but feeling something doesn't make it true. I am loved and valued. How do I know? Because God told me so. He tells me in His Word that He loves me and cares for me. That alone ought to make me realize my worth to Him.

God is calling us to take a walk of faith. That walk will continue to be filled with hurts, rejections, and all kinds of unpleasant things. The only way we can step into that faith realm is if we stop reacting to everything with our emotions. Now there's a challenge! Because we are human, our emotions are tough to fight against. However, it's absolutely essential that we hand over our emotions to the Lord and stand on what we believe about who He is rather than put our trust in how we "feel." Emotions can't be trusted; only He can be trusted.

Part of our problem is that we live in a society that tells us to do whatever our "hearts" tell us to do. If we like something, take it! If something doesn't make us feel OK, don't do it, or get rid of it—or divorce it. Advertisements scream at us on all fronts, flirting with our senses, and catering to our emotions. We tend to trust our emotions way too much. We need to let go of them, but we are encouraged to pamper them instead.

I've had to face new feelings of rejection that I never would have if my husband hadn't left. But because he did, and because I wanted companionship, for a few years I stepped out of my comfort zone and attempted to meet new people—not necessarily with the intent of marrying, but at least to find someone I would enjoy going out with for dinner or a concert or whatever. I had no idea what I was getting myself into.

I'm no longer the sweet young thing that men could've been attracted to thirty—even twenty—years ago. I may feel the same, but after taking a good, long look at myself in the mirror (not, mind you, after I first crawl out of bed in the morning, or the shock might be too much for my heart!). I've had to face the reality that what used to take ten minutes to "fix up" now takes an hour, and then I have to be very careful that I haven't in my enthusiasm applied so much make-up that I look like I just crawled out of the crypt!

Unfortunately for most women of my age, most men of my age (and even older) have somehow aged in a different way. Men look "distinguished," or at least have aged much more gracefully than we women have. Maybe because of that fact they also seem to be more interested in the younger models when looking for a date. Wow. What a surprise that is, right?

At first, I was pretty depressed by this fact. I had taken the advice of my kids (I should know better) and subscribed to an online Christian dating service. In my line of work, it is very difficult to meet people, so it seemed logical. I wasn't looking for marriage—just friendship. What's the harm in that? Nothing—at least, that's what I thought until I found out that a lot of men out there are looking for something entirely different. I posted a couple of pictures that I thought were pretty good of myself. I included the usual little bio that is a requirement for such dating sites. I sat back and waited. I waited. Then I waited some more.

Eventually, I actually conversed with a few people. But, all in all, I was rejected quite a bit. My intention was to find a nice,

Christian man who had similar beliefs and wasn't afraid to admit it. But for quite some time, my old insecurities told me that I must be some kind of hideous-looking old woman that no man in his right mind would even consider for a date!

I'll never forget the Saturday I received notice through this service that I had been "matched" with a very nice-looking man about my age who really sounded interesting. He was pretty cute. "OK," I thought, "stay calm. Just wait a few hours to communicate. Don't look too anxious here." When I finally decided that I'd given it enough time and I should send some questions to him, the man had "closed" the match! No nice little message was sent. Nothing. He'd obviously taken one look and clicked the "Close Match" button. What a reality check that gave me!

Another time, a man had sent me a couple of emails and, I thought, seemed interested. I waited a few days to answer one of his notes, and when I finally wrote back, he responded something like this: "Look, I don't mean to offend you, but to tell you the truth, I get so many emails on a daily basis from women that I honestly don't even know who you are!" He'd either forgotten me in the brief few days since we'd last communicated, or was a complete jerk and thought it was cute to be insulting. Whatever the case, I stopped checking my messages for a couple of weeks.

I really felt defeated. Who was I kidding, anyway? I would never find what I'd once had with my ex-husband. I felt embarrassed and foolish. Hadn't the rejection of my ex-husband been enough for me? Did I really have to go out looking for more of the same from total strangers?

Then a light slowly turned on in my brain. I began to let that man's words really sink into my brain: "I don't even know who you are." He was exactly right. He had no clue whatsoever. But, to my amazement, I finally realized that it would be his loss, not mine.

You see, I do know who I am now. The fact that he didn't just wasn't important, after all. Knowing who I am gave me the confidence that if someone else didn't want to know me, then that was OK, because it didn't make me any less valid as a human being.

For the first time, perhaps, I found out I actually liked myself. Yes, there are little things I'd like to change, but I know I'm willing to work on my faults and weaknesses while accepting my strengths and personality. It's taken me sixty-two years now to finally appreciate it. I can look in the mirror and, despite the flaws, see a happy, whole, and complete person. I honestly like who I've become. God's given me some insight into the kind of person I am, and how He's used me just where I am—warts and all. I guess that's better than a lot of people can say.

Author and talk show host Tavis Smiley wrote, "Take your focus off how others see you. Cease being obsessed with the need to impress. Don't allow the approval of others to obstruct your view of yourself."[7] In other words, stop trying to seek validation through other people. Better yet, don't let other people (except for God) tell you who you are or what you're worth.

Unfortunately, so many marriages end up in divorce because people have entered into those marriages for just that reason, and when the other person no longer makes them "feel" good, they move on to someone else. The cycle goes on, over and over again.

I don't know if God will permit me to find someone to share the rest of my life with, but I've decided not to become obsessed with it. It's in His hands, which is where it should be. I know He hasn't forgotten where I am. He's still there, watching over me. He is the mirror I choose to see myself in.

Here are a couple of Scriptures I think you will find helpful if you're struggling to overcome insecurity.

> Then the word of the Lord came to me, saying: "Before I formed you in the womb I knew you; before you were born I sanctified you. I ordained you a prophet to the nations."

---

7. "Leadership Empowerment Week: Whose Approval Are You Seeking?" SYS Ministries, Inc., Aug. 14, 2012.

Then I said, "Ah, Lord God! Behold, I cannot speak, for I am a youth."

But the Lord said to me: "Do not say, 'I am youth,' for you shall go to all to whom I send you, and whatever I command you, you shall speak. Do not be afraid of their faces, for I am with you to deliver you," says the Lord.

—Jer. 1:4-8

Then Moses said to the Lord, "O my Lord, I am not eloquent, neither before nor since You have spoken to your servant; but I am slow of speech and slow of tongue."

So the Lord said to him, "Who has made man's mouth? Or who makes the mute, the deaf, the seeing, or the blind? Have not I, the Lord? Now therefore, go, and I will be with your mouth and teach you what You shall say."

—Ex. 4:10-12

Chapter 9

NO LONGER A VICTIM

A bruised reed He will not break, and smoking flax He will not quench, till He sends forth justice to victory.

— Matt. 12:20

From the shadows extending outside the window, you know you need to eat something and get ready to settle in for the night. You find a few heavy blankets on a shelf, which is good, since you've no way to start a fire. There's one last granola bar and a bag of nuts left in your knapsack. At least you still have a couple of bottles of water. You try to ignore the rumblings of your empty stomach and promise it that it will be rewarded if you ever get out of this predicament.

You bed down on the hard, but dry, floor with the blankets. It's that, or the hard chair with your feet propped up against the window sill, and the chair doesn't seem to offer much in the comfort department. It looks as if it may be on its last leg. You fear that should you try to sleep in it, it might come crashing down before morning!

After much fluffing of the not-so-clean blankets and finding the exact position for a knapsack pillow, you finally sprawl on the floor with a private wish for no little critters to join you.

Sometime in the night, you dream you're standing in the middle of a field and are suddenly lifted by strong and capable wings—or were they arms?—high above the ground. Such *freedom!* High above the scene below, through valleys, and up again to the heights of the mountains, you fly. You turn to see that a majestic eagle has you safe in the shadow of his wings.

The vision was so vivid, and the sensation of flying so incredibly real, that it takes you several moments to figure out where you are when you wake up. It's still the middle of the night. Normally your heart would be racing, but you know you are loved and that God will lift you above not only your present circumstances, but also above your problems. You no longer feel like a victim of your situation. You begin to see that, instead, God has been trying to teach you something through it. You sense, for the first time, that you're getting stronger because of these past couple days. You know that you are finally hearing from God! He is with you, and now you feel more confident than ever that your decision to come this direction was directed by Him to bring you closer to getting home. Instead of frustration, you begin to feel a thankfulness welling up inside you. You're not alone after all!

For the first time, you feel as if you are part of a bigger plan and that, though you blamed God for all the chaos, He still has a purpose for your existence and experiences, no matter how painful they may be.

One of the hardest things to do when you're facing the end of your marriage is to avoid the victim mentality. So many things are thrown at you at once that sometimes it's hard to keep up with it all. You sometimes feel that the world is against you—for good reason, one might argue—making it easy to feel sorry for yourself.

For example, a friend of mine is going through a divorce right now. Like me, she was married to her husband for many years—almost thirty. He, too, committed adultery. They have grown children, just as we did at the time of our divorce. So many similarities. The differences lie in the circumstances: she found out after all those years that he is gay. The affair he had was with another man. Not only is she having to deal with that news, which nearly broke her, but the divorce is now dragging on, with him trying to keep his financial worth secret so as to keep most of their money and assets for himself. To call it a nightmare is an understatement—in many ways, it's much worse than anything I faced. She's weary, and many days she tells me she can't take much more.

When facing such pain, it is no wonder that we begin to feel like a victim of our circumstances. I know that God wants her to rise above her storm, just as He did me and anyone else suffering through divorce, but it's a struggle. No two divorces are alike, and therefore we all deal with different battles. The common denominator to all is the fact that it threatens to take us out as Christians unless we are firmly planted in our relationship with God. One way we're taken out is when we start having the "poor me" attitude. He wants us to live victoriously, but it's hard to do that when we have so much hurt and trauma to deal with. How do we do it? A better question is, "How do we keep a good attitude and keep from taking on a victim mentality?" Is it even possible when everything in our life seems to be falling apart?

It's His plan for us to rise up from the ashes with a renewed vision for the future and renewed purpose. I have to believe that in order to get there, keeping a good attitude is the key. As Joyce Meyer says in her book *Battlefield of the Mind*, "Patience is not the ability to wait, it is the ability to keep a good attitude while waiting."[8] That's hard enough a task when circumstances around us are normal, but if our life is a war zone with the casualties of that war strewn everywhere around us, it's a much more difficult task to accomplish.

---

8. Joyce Meyer, *Battlefield of the Mind: Winning the Battle in Your Mind* (Nashville: Faith Words, 1999), 213.

Almost two years to the month after my husband left me, I wrote these words in my journal: "Surely, Lord, there's a plan for my future too, right? This can't be all there is. Lord, help me to rest in You, to wait on You, and be content that You have all this under control. I pray You're not finished working in any of these situations I'm dealing with yet, right?" Obviously, I was questioning God because although I know what the Word promises, I was not seeing much improvement in my circumstances and was wondering if my ship was indeed going to sink! It had been two years, and still I was struggling. What happens when our struggle lasts for years and years, as is the case with many divorces? What then?

I have prayed to be more like Joseph in this area, because despite the circumstances that surrounded his life, the Bible speaks of him as being someone with an "excellent spirit." This, despite being sold out by his brothers and taken into slavery, then imprisoned under false accusations. His life was basically derailed at the young age of seventeen. It took over thirteen years of slavery and then imprisonment before God restored his life and the promises He'd given him were fulfilled. Perhaps we have to be in a position of brokenness before He can use us, and our disappointments actually serve to grow us spiritually. Maybe that is the key to finally finding purpose in the things we face.

Another way to battle the victim mentality is by waiting: waiting on God, waiting for His timing for answers to prayer, waiting for opportunities He might have for me. Waiting can be a problem when facing various setbacks in our lives, but we need to remember that our setbacks can become God's opportunities! When we remember that, it helps keep us from getting discouraged. In her book *How to Succeed at Being Yourself*, Joyce Meyer says, "according to Psalm 31:15 my times are in His hands. God knows the exact time that is right for everything, and none of our impatience is going to rush Him."[9] That was my struggle,

---

9. Joyce Meyer, *How to Succeed at Being Yourself: Finding Confidence to Fulfill Your Destiny* (New York: Warner Faith, 1999), 89.

and is the struggle of all of us walking through divorce. We're disappointed. Things didn't work out the way they were supposed to, and now we find ourselves in a holding pattern waiting to see what happens next! What will we do with our lives now? Waiting wouldn't be so bad, except sometimes what we're waiting for takes longer than we'd like it to. We'd like for things to change in our lives right away.

We need to remember that God might be wanting to form something in us *while* we wait that will be necessary for us further down the road. Just as Joseph wasn't ready to do what God wanted him to do as a seventeen-year-old, we too might have to go through some preparation in order to perform the task He has for us in life. In a sermon entitled "The Wait Room of God," my pastor, Randy Harvey of The Crossing Church in The Woodlands, said that we may have had a "Plan A" that didn't work out (like my marriage to my husband), but the "Plan B" we find ourselves living now may turn out to be what God intended for us all along. Meanwhile, He may be working on our "root system." Without a strong root system, a plant is weak—and so are we.

Scriptures tell us how to deal with waiting. They tell us to give thanks despite what we're facing or how we're feeling. They even suggest we thank Him in our circumstances. That is the key to having a right attitude and an excellent spirit! As it says in 1 Thessalonians 5:16-18, "Rejoice always; pray without ceasing; in *everything* give thanks; for this is the will of God in Christ Jesus for you" (italics added). Like most people, I find it hard to be thankful for someone breaking my heart, walking away, and leaving me alone! And how can that possibly be His will for any of us? While it's nearly impossible to thank Him for those things, I know that it *is* possible to thank God despite what's happening around me, and to thank Him for what He will do in me while walking through life's storms. Nothing dismisses our urge to play the victim quite like taking a position of being thankful. You can't feel sorry for yourself while you're thanking God!

Begin by taking inventory of all the blessings in your life. If we concentrate on what we've lost instead of what we still have, it will cripple us. I'm reminded of one of my very favorite Christmas movies, *It's a Wonderful Life*, which is about a man who sacrifices his whole life to help others. Because of someone else's terrible mistake, he loses a large amount of money that means almost certain bankruptcy. In utter despair and with seemingly no way out of the mess he's in, he wishes he'd never been born. An angel helps him to see what life would've been like, were he granted this wish. He's able to see that he indeed has lived a wonderful life and was a blessed man. Not only was he blessed, he'd blessed others—a fact that, because of the calamity of his circumstances and his view of the events, he was unable to see or understand before.

We can be just like that when we are going through something as devastating as a divorce. We can't see the good all around us because we're looking only at the bad, so we have to stop and take inventory of all we still have. We have to change our perspective on things. Once we change our focus and look upon all our blessings, we can truly begin to be thankful again.

It helps to surrender our expectations. We have developed the belief, albeit unrealistic, that God will take us out of our troubles. There is a false belief that if we are born-again believers, life should be a fairytale in which everything turns out happily-ever-after. He never promised us that. He said we would face troubling circumstances, but He would walk with us through them. In order to keep our attitude right, we have to understand that our own expectations will cause us much frustration, and in the end we will stay upset if things aren't working out the way we wanted them to. We need to bow to His sovereignty over our lives and lay down our expectations at His feet. Nothing feels as freeing.

The next thing we need to realize, if we're going to maintain a good attitude, is that our waiting needs to be proactive. Waiting doesn't mean we just sit back and do nothing. Joseph, when he found himself in slavery, sold out by his brothers, decided to become the best slave he could be. He found favor with his master and was given great responsibility because, apparently, he was no slouch in his work! He could've become angry and bitter over what had happened to him and been negligent in his work, but instead, he decided to use this time to hone better character skills. When imprisoned because of the false accusations of Potiphar's wife, he became a model prisoner, gaining favor with the chief jailer. It's interesting to note that Joseph, always the dreamer, was used by God to interpret the dreams of others during his time in prison. This, eventually, led to his promotion later on. He made the choice somewhere along the way that his circumstances weren't going to keep him down—he would use them for God's glory. As a result, in Genesis 45:8, this is what he could say to his brothers in the end when he finally faced them after many years of separation: "So now it was not you who sent me here, but God; and He has made me a father to Pharaoh, and lord of all his house, and a ruler throughout all the land of Egypt." Now that's what I call a good attitude and an excellent spirit. He was able to see that a devastating blow in his life became the way for God to promote him and accomplish His will for his life. I think he would've agreed with Psalm 119:71, 72: "It is a good thing that I have been afflicted that I may learn Your statutes. The law of Your mouth is better to me than thousands of coins of gold and silver."

Joseph had the right values. If we have the right values, when adversity comes, our values will be our anchor. We need to cling to them like a faithful friend so that they can help give us direction instead of causing us to lose our direction in life. When we lose our direction, we face a crisis. Dr. James Dobson said, "Whenever we build our lives on values and principles that contradict the time-honored wisdom of God's Words, we are laying a foundation on the sand. Sooner or later the storms will howl and the structure we have laboriously constructed will collapse with a mighty crash."[10] We need to ask ourselves what our core values

---

10. *Dr. James Dobson's Family Talk*, "Avoiding a Midlife Crisis", 2016.

are. If they are centered on Christ, they will help us keep the attitude right when we are faced with abandonment, separation, or the end of a marriage.

The final tool to battle victimization is keeping our dreams alive. I know that there were many dreams I had when I was younger. When my husband divorced me, I confess that, for a while, anyway, I gave up on many of those dreams. I felt that they were no longer possible. In a way, I disqualified myself from life. Partly it was due to the sadness I felt. I just lost interest in life. But, along with that, I believed that I was "taken out" of the game of life. Benched. No longer a valuable player. I was allowing the disappointment of my divorce to define who I was. I felt myself slipping down the slope toward quitting. It really is true that without vision, people perish. I was on my way there, for I found that I had stopped dreaming.

All my life I wanted to write, but I never seemed to get around to it. First it was because I was working full time. Then I was busy raising my family. It just never seemed to happen. It took losing my husband to finally come full circle, back to something I've always loved and wanted to do. The very pain that nearly broke me has been the launching pad for my passion. In that sense, it was all worth it. The loss was the very thing that gave me back my dream.

We need to fight for our dreams, and on days when we feel like giving up, we need to dig in and stand firm, not give up on them. I heard someone say once, "The test of endurance comes at the point of quitting!" If we want to endure and rise above what happened in our marriages and in our lives, we can't quit. We need to discern these moments of life-changing decisions, so that we have the sense to move beyond what has become our "norm" and into a future that only God can make possible! We are much like that smoking flax in the Scripture: "A bruised reed He will not break, and smoking flax He will not quench, till He sends forth justice to victory" (Matt. 12:20). When a candle is blown out, it resembles us when we've been "taken out" by the circumstances of life, like in a divorce. Our "fire" has been snuffed out. But if we allow God to do it, He can breathe on us and set the embers on fire again, just like putting oxygen on that wick. He can cause us to dream again. It's what He desires for us.

The only way to get a new vision for our life after divorce is to pursue Him again with everything we've got. It's time to get up and start living again. Turn from the former things and reach for something new. When Joseph was young, he was a dreamer, but his dreams were for a future time. It took years for those dreams to be fulfilled, and he had to go through much suffering to get there. Fortunately, he kept his faith and never forgot what God had spoken to him years before. He knew God had a plan for him. He didn't allow himself to play the victim or feel sorry for himself.

Some of those dreams we had many years ago could still come to pass, and we need to pick them up again. Just because our marriages failed, it doesn't mean we're disqualified from those dreams coming true. Joseph had to wait thirteen years. Moses waited forty. Abraham and Sarah waited twenty-five, and Jesus waited thirty. Don't give up on your dreams. It may just be that God wants you to grow and mature in ways that you never thought possible, and until you do, your dreams can't come to fruition.

I love the fact that we're really never too old to accomplish our dreams. The only thing holding us back is ourselves. The Bible is filled with stories of people who, at a very old age, were called to do something new. A couple of years ago when I was contemplating retirement, I was on a walk at a neighborhood park. There I heard the Lord's voice say to me, "Behold, I will do a new thing; even now it shall spring forth. Will you not know it?" Boom. A dream was reborn in me; and within the next year, I was on my way to having this book published. Just like Joseph, I could finally see a purpose in all the waiting and all the struggle and pain I'd gone through. It has put in me a thankfulness for my circumstances.

In order to keep a good attitude and not develop a victim mentality, we must first learn to be thankful for the struggles we've found ourselves in and seek to find out what God is trying to accomplish through them. Then we need to give up on our expectations of what should and shouldn't be happening in our lives, for it only causes us frustration. Next, we should decide to be proactive in our waiting. We must wait with purpose, and find what it is we can be doing while we wait. Let our values be our anchor that keeps us from losing our direction during the storms of life. And learn to dream again. Stir up old dreams and search for new ones that can keep us moving forward instead of letting our divorce define us.

Here are some Scriptures that will encourage you to move forward with the right attitude.

> Therefore, be patient brethren, until the coming of the Lord. See how the farmer waits for the precious fruit of the earth, waiting patiently for it until it receives early and latter rain. You also be patient. Establish your hearts, for the coming of the Lord is at hand.
>
> —Jam. 5:7, 8

> Blessed is the man whose strength is in You, whose heart is set on pilgrimage. As they pass through the Valley of Baca [weeping, pain, hurts], they make it a spring; the rain also covers it with pools. They go from strength to strength.
>
> —Psa. 84:5-7a

> Do not remember the former things nor consider the things of old. Behold, I will do a new thing. Now it shall spring forth. Shall you not know it? I will even make a road in the wilderness and rivers in the desert.
>
> —Isa. 43:18, 19

Rejoice always, pray without ceasing. In everything give thanks, for this is the will of God in Christ Jesus for you. Do not quench the Spirit. Do not despise prophecies. Test all things; hold fast to what is good. Abstain from every form of evil.

—1 Thess. 5:16-22

Write the vision and make it plain on tablets, that he may run who reads it. For the vision is yet for an appointed time; but at the end it will speak and it will not lie. Though it tarries, wait for it, because it will surely come; it will not tarry.

—Hab. 2:2b, 3

Commit your works to the Lord, and your thoughts will be established.

—Prov. 16:3

Blessed is the man who trusts in the Lord, and whose hope is the Lord. For he shall be like a tree planted by the waters, which spreads out its roots by the river, and will not fear when heat comes; But its leaf will be green, and will not be anxious in the year of the drought, nor will cease from yielding fruit.

—Jer. 17:7, 8

It is good that one should hope and wait quietly for the salvation of the Lord.

—Lam. 3:26

It is a good thing that I have been afflicted that I may learn Your statutes. The law of Your mouth is better to me than thousands of coins of gold and silver.

—Psa. 119:71, 72

And not only that, but we also glory in tribulations, knowing that tribulation produces perseverance; and perseverance, character and character, hope.

—Rom. 5:3, 4

I will sing to the Lord as long as I live; I will sing praise to my God while I have my being. May my meditations be sweet to Him; I will be glad in the Lord.

—Psa. 104:33, 34

And the desire of the righteous will be granted. When the whirlwind passes by . . . the righteous have an everlasting foundation.

—Prov. 10:25

I wait for the Lord, my soul waits, And in His word I do hope. My soul waits for the Lord more than those who watch for the morning—yes, more than those who watch for the morning.

—Psa. 130:5

Let integrity and uprightness preserve me, for I wait for You.

—Psa. 25:21

Chapter 10
FOLLOW THE PATH

> For the vision is yet for an appointed time; but at the end it will speak, and it will not lie. Though it tarries, wait for it; because it will surely come, it will not tarry.
>
> —Hab. 2:3

You slowly get up, feeling every muscle scream from the strain of the last few days' hiking and the night on the hard floor, but you aren't complaining. You were warmer last night than all of the last few nights put together, and you're grateful for the little shelter. There is a warmth inside you so deep that you can only explain it as God's healing. When you think about how you felt only a couple of days before, you know you're a different person.

Your stomach growls, and you're ravenous. You ate the last granola bar, so you're left with nuts and your last water bottle. You pray that somehow you'll find your way out today, and you won't need anything else.

You hobble over to the window and stand there several moments, thinking about how far you've travelled in the past couple of days—not just in the woods but in your relationship with God. Your earlier feelings of anger are replaced with an unexplainable peace.

You check your maps, hoping that they will shed some light on your whereabouts. They are still damp, but not too bad. The water damage has smeared the ink to the point that it is impossible to make any sense of it. You toss them in the corner.

After a quick prayer and a moment of listening for God's direction, you step onto the front porch. You look back once, feeling that it was nothing short of a miracle to have found a shelter for the night—proof of God's hand. You whisper a thank-you to Him for His provision and set off down the path.

After a few hours, you start feeling that familiar fear, but you push it aside because this is the way you're compelled to go. Nothing is recognizable, and you suspect that you're getting farther and farther away from the river and from your campsite. Why would God send you this way? It's at moments like this that you wish for an audible voice to say, "This is the way! Yes, that's right. A little further to the left. Now go right. Only a little farther and you'll see where I'm taking you!" But only the silence of the forest greets you.

Then you hear it. At first it's a slight pounding, but as you continue forward, it grows louder and louder until you're sure it must be just ahead and to the left of the trail. Feeling desperate to find out the source, you quicken your steps, only to find that your ankle, now throbbing again, won't allow it. As you come to the top of a small rise in the path, you look down and hear a cry escape your mouth. There is smoke rising from a cabin, bigger than the little shed you spent the night in. Next to the cabin is a man taking wood from a pile and placing it on a chopping block. You watch as he lifts his arms above his head and swings his axe down, severing it in two.

You try to move downhill toward the cabin, but your legs and feet have turned to jelly. You find it hard to go on. You collapse, but not before crying out, hoping that the man can hear your weak call.

You wake with a start to find yourself lying in bed in a room you've never seen before, covered with an old, handmade quilt. There are signs of a woman's touch in the decorative details of the room, and an obvious designer's eye for color and texture. Despite knowing deep down that it belongs to a stranger, you feel welcome and at home here.

There is a light knocking at the door, and you say, "Come in." The door opens for the same man you saw outside chopping wood earlier.

He seems hesitant. "I'm sorry," he says. "I didn't mean to bother you. I only wanted to check in. You've been out for about an hour. I didn't see a bump on your head or anything, so I didn't see the need to take you into town right away. Looked like exhaustion, nothing some rest wouldn't help."

It takes some time to unravel the last few days to your host, but he allows you to take it. He leads you to the kitchen and presents you a cup of coffee and the biggest plate of food you've seen in a while! In between bites, you tell him about the frightening night in the storm and the days of confusion that followed, along with how you've been injured and found the little shed. He listens with patience, as if he has all the time in the world.

"Does that shed belong to you?" you have to ask.

He pauses for a moment and seems to prepare himself before answering. "Yes, or that is, it used to. I haven't been there in years. I used it as a place to stay back when I went hunting occasionally."

It's clear now that you've been on this man's land for some time. He is a widower who lost his wife to cancer a few years before. His daughter, he tells you with obvious sadness, was killed in a car accident when she was fifteen. You remember them both from the picture you saw in the cabin.

He has clearly lived in pain for many years. You sense it in his voice.

He stops, and it takes a few moments for him to be able to speak again. "The area you say you were camping in was completely flooded," he said after a while. "In fact, if you'd continued on your path leading back to the campsite, you would've run into high water." You realize this would've caused you to backtrack several miles and delayed you even more. God really was looking out for you!

As the afternoon passes and you gradually gain your strength, it becomes time for him to take you to your car. You've been touched by his story, and feel a strange connection with the man you just met. On the drive, you think about your compass, now broken and in pieces. It represents all the things you used to put your trust in, the control you once thought you had of your own life.

When the man stops his car next to yours, you pull out the broken compass and give it to him. "God helped me find my way because of a broken compass. He can help you find yours again too."

❦ ❦ ❦ ❦

In a perfect world, my life would be very different from what it is right now. I would be facing my retirement years with the man I married forty years ago. Retirement wouldn't be nearly as scary financially as it can sometimes be for me now living on my income as a former educator. We'd be spending weekends riding his motorcycle around, maybe visiting scenic Texas locations, stopping by roadside cafes, looking through antique stores, just "hanging out"—together.

When home, we'd be with our kids and grandkids, grilling hamburgers, entertaining by the pool I no longer have at the house I no longer own, watching the grandkids as normal grandparents do—together. As it is, I do get to spend precious time with my children and grandchildren, and I've been blessed to live close enough to them that our visits are frequent. It makes me sad to know that he forfeited that time with them, and I wish, for their sake, it was a different set of circumstances.

There would also be the yearly vacations, skiing in the winter with the family, maybe a trip through Texas hill country or to the Florida beaches in the summer. That's what we did all those many years ago. Christmases with the family, laughing over the same old stories about loved ones who have passed.

Life would be easier. Or at least it would seem easier, because I wouldn't be living it alone. My kids wouldn't have to face the disappointment of losing the dad they'd expected to be here for them. My grandchildren would know their grandfather better. Relationships would still be intact.

My bank account would be fuller. My bills wouldn't seem as large. Don't get me wrong— God has answered all my financial needs, one by one—but going from a two-income household to a single income household so suddenly has definitely presented its challenges for me through the years.

We all have an idea of how life should be, don't we? We all have a desire to have it all, whatever that means to each of us. I can remember, in my teen years, having a very idealistic view of the world, despite my family situation and my insecurities. At the time, I guess I called it optimistic. I believed that things would work out for my good, even if I had to endure an occasional hardship. I still tend to believe in the best in most situations. At least I hope I do on most issues. Unfortunately, we all have to face setbacks.

I looked forward to finding Mr. Right, settling down, having 2.5 children (how exactly are we supposed to achieve that?), finding the perfect house on the perfect street, going to the perfect job, and living a perfectly comfortable life. It's what we all wish for.

In thinking about this one day, I remembered a conversation I had with one of my best friends back in the fall of '73. Jack was one of those people I felt close to during my high school days. His parents were giving me a ride to Springfield, Missouri, that fall, because I was going to attend the same college as he was. I'd stayed home a year after graduation to work and earn some money, still indecisive about what college to attend or even if I would go to college at all. Now my mind was made up, and I knew that I wanted to study to become a teacher.

We'd driven from Sioux City, Iowa, to Springfield that day, ready to embark on a new adventure in our lives. Jack, like me, was trying to find his way in life. It was tough leaving home, at least for me. I was the last of Mom's four kids to leave her. When I looked back at her from that van window and saw her small frame standing in the doorway of our modest duplex, waving goodbye to me, it took everything in me to keep from bursting into tears and jumping from that moving van. This was what I wanted, but I hated leaving Mom behind. She was that anchor that had held everything together my whole life. What could I possibly do without her?

I was not unlike millions of other young people as they leave home to venture out into the world, but, to me, that moment was strictly personal. Mom had done her job with me; now it was my turn to take over as an adult on my own. As I rode on silently that day, so many memories of home invaded my thinking. Surprisingly, as the miles stretched between home and that van, I began feeling the strength she'd given me all those years. Deep down inside, though hungry for home already, I began to sense that this was one of the most important decisions of my life—going away to college—and I knew I would somehow be all right.

That evening we all stayed at a motel in Springfield. The college was closed by the time we arrived, so we had to wait until the next day to go get registered and settled into our dorms. So many thoughts were going through my head that I knew I'd have a hard time sleeping. More than any other thing, I was aware that this was the first time I'd ever ventured away from home my whole life. I was leaving everything I loved and was familiar with. It was exhilarating yet terrifying at the same time.

Apparently, Jack was feeling the same way, although the separation from parents hadn't hit him yet. His parents left the next day. We found ourselves sitting outside by the motel pool, talking about everything that was about to happen to us the next day. As we were talking, I realized something else. We would each likely be branching out into many new friendships, and to an extent, I felt like I was about to say goodbye—literally, perhaps—to this good friend as well. Jack and I had grown up together in the same church and had come to be close friends during high school. We had belonged to the same youth group, shared the same circle of friends, and known each other well.

I hoped we would remain friends, but sadly, we would lose touch with each other in the years after we left college. We would end up going our separate ways, as is the case with most childhood friendships. I could sense all this that night—that nothing would ever be the same. How right I was.

As we sat and shared our feelings about this new chapter in our lives, our hopes, our fears, and losing what we'd left behind in our hometown, including the people we most cared about, our conversation began to focus on finding God's will for ourselves. It's funny. I know for a fact that this was what we talked about, though I don't remember the specifics of what was said or what our conclusions were. Maybe that's because neither one of us really knew the answer completely, did we? Here we were, about to step out into our futures, but the truth was that God's will was part of an ongoing process. We were just at the brink of finding it. I think we were both somewhat apprehensive of the future, but I can still remember that giddy feeling of anticipation that one has when they're about to set out on an adventure.

The next four years were some of the best of my life. When it was over, I looked back with a great sense of nostalgia on those days at Evangel University. New friendships and new experiences laced with my newly found freedom gave me such a feeling of expectancy over the next few years. The sky was the limit. I could do anything I set my mind to.

The decisions to make were endless, as it turned out. Each day presented its challenges, questions, and possibilities. When I think back, I realize my life could have taken so many different roads. So many choices were made. I wonder what might've happened had I not made the ones I did. Yet those very choices became a part of who I am today. Were it not for those choices, both then and ever since, I couldn't possibly have turned into the person I am now. I don't regret any of them—even the choice of a partner, though he eventually walked away from our life together. Even so, I can now look back with gratitude on the choices I made.

As I contemplate those college years, something else comes to mind as well. It seemed as if I had forever ahead of me. It was as though time didn't matter at all. Ah, the joy of youth, right? It's only as age begins to creep up on us that we begin to realize how short our time on this earth really is. Suddenly ten, twenty, thirty, forty or more years go by and we wake up to realize that our life is slipping away. While all this time is vanishing into thin air, we begin to develop a feeling of urgency. At one point we believed we had all the time in the world to accomplish our goals; then it appears we might never be able to attain them before the last grains of sand in the hourglass of our life fall.

No wonder so many men and women my age suffer from midlife crises! If we don't hurry up, we'll wake up to find that there's no time left at all, and we'll have missed out. Or so we think. Many people begin some pretty bizarre things that are totally out-of-character—like selling everything they have to go live in a commune on top of a mountain, or going on a massive shopping spree with their retirement money—or maybe finding someone twenty years younger than they are to help them feel younger. It's almost like having an identity crisis that so many young people go through before they mature and find their place in life.

I think the problem lies partly within ourselves and partly in all the wrong messages that this world sends out to us through the media, newspapers, books, you name it. Here in America, probably more so than in any other country in the world, we all seem to be on a quest to find ourselves. We're encouraged to do whatever it takes to make the almighty "me" happy, even at the expense of those around us. We're constantly being told that we have to look out for our *own* interests, our *own* wants, needs, and desires—when God's Word clearly states that it's only when we lose our life that we actually gain it.

For me, my "change" was compounded by the fact that at forty-eight I felt like half of me was suddenly missing. Together, my husband and I had made a whole, completed picture—maybe not a perfect picture, but a picture nonetheless. Now I felt incomplete, and I no longer knew how the picture was even supposed to look.

The Word clearly tells us that in marriage, we become as one person. This is the problem many people have nowadays in marriage relationships, considering society encourages us to be much more self-seeking in our thinking. That's what the natural order of things is, though. God is the head of man. Man, in marriage, is the head of woman. (Sorry girls, but the Bible is pretty clear here. You know where I'm going with this.) My life had become enmeshed with my husband's. We, together, had made the whole. Two very different people had come together to form a bond that should have stayed solid.

Everything I became from that time on existed within the framework of that marriage. He became my best friend. He became my confidante. His wishes became my desires. His dreams were my dreams and vice-versa. For twenty-five years, if you'd asked me to define who I was, I would most likely have answered you in terms of who I was in my marriage first and then as a mother—*then* I would probably have told you about myself, personally. I still was that same person I was before I married, but after all those years with my husband, I had a hard time separating myself from our marriage, even after he had proclaimed it to be over.

After the divorce, I was discovering myself all over again, just as I had in college. I had to reacquaint myself with me. I wasn't used to thinking as a separate entity from my husband, and I had a hard time adjusting to the idea. It felt unnatural and uncomfortable. As time has passed, however, instead of the idea frightening me, it's actually led to my metamorphosis. I have felt sometimes like a caterpillar going through all its changes to become a beautiful butterfly. At times, I try to stay in my cocoon, to forego the entire procedure. But a caterpillar has to deal with the uncomfortable in order to become a beautiful butterfly. We can only become that through Christ and His working in us.

God has reintroduced me to myself, in a way. Some things I've learned about myself have been positive, and some have been negative. I said before that I've finally come to like myself. That's a positive.

There are things about me, however, that I'm learning are not so great. Those things I've had to turn over to the Lord, and I'll continue to have to do that, I'm afraid. My apparent lack of organizational skills, my tendency to procrastinate, my tendency to fear change and cling to what I'm used to instead of embracing new experiences, and my ever-reappearing lack of confidence are just a few. I laugh too loud at the wrong things, when I should be more serious, and vice-versa. I waste time on trivial things, worry too much over things I can do nothing about, and obsess over things that should be no-brainers.

But along with the negatives, God has shown me some positive things to build upon. For one thing, I've found that I'm good at encouraging others—if I allow God to work through me. I've learned that I enjoy people. I love to laugh and make other people laugh with me. Because of that, there was a brief time that I decided to help with greeting people on Sunday mornings at church—another thing that I wouldn't have done a few years ago. I found out that I'm basically a loyal, trustworthy friend, and if you're my friend, you can count on me to be there for you. I have a desire to share my testimony with other people who are going through difficult times similar to mine. Divorces are an ever-increasing number, unfortunately, and will continue to rise until the Lord's return. It's the hour we live in.

I'm learning that the more I open myself up to Him, the more He'll direct my path. I used to try to hurry things up in regard to discovering where God wants my life to go, but I'm finding that it's a more gradual process, and a day-by-day lesson in trust. More than anything else, I'm learning that I have to shut out the outside noises that battle for my attention—whether it's work, family, the media, anything, really, that takes the place of communion with Him.

Many years ago, God taught me a very valuable lesson in this. I had been on my own since my daughter had moved out, got married, and started building a life with her new husband and my grandson. My son, his wife, and my two-year-old grandson had been living with me, saving up to buy their own home. It's funny, but although I'd been divorced since fall of 2002, I'd never really lived alone, except for the three-month period my daughter and other grandson were out of the house and on their own. Then, after two years of living with me, my son and his wife finally found a house and moved into it. In some ways, I was ready. Not that I was happy to see them go, but it was time. They needed to be able to start a home away from Mom. They needed their privacy—all couples need that in order to grow closer.

But when the last load of their belongings was moved out and they stood on the back step saying goodbye, I felt as if I was about to explode into tears. It was silly, really, considering they would be only fifteen minutes away from me! I felt ridiculous, yet couldn't help myself. The realization had finally come that I had the house completely to myself, and neither of my kids would be coming home again to dwell there with me. It reminded me of when my own mom stood in the doorway of her duplex, waving goodbye to the last of her children going off to college. Now I understood the feelings she must've had.

For the first time ever, all the little things that I had done as a mom for my family had ceased to be necessary. No longer did I have to worry about cooking dinner. I didn't have to go to the grocery store every few days to pick up food. I found one meal could stretch out over an entire week! I didn't have to clean house every weekend, and I realized if I didn't clean it, who would care? (That, of course, was a plus!)

After a few weeks of this, a very depressing sense of no longer being needed fell over me. I couldn't shake it. I felt the "empty nest" syndrome in full force. I came in from work every day to an empty house with the knowledge that, unless God brings another person into my life, this could be the way it will be for the next thirty or forty years! It was, in a sense, a delayed response to my divorce—I no longer had the companionship of my children to soften the blow.

One Saturday morning, I woke up with that same empty feeling of "OK, it's just me again with nothing to look forward to" gnawing in my gut. I began missing the days when the kids were young, remembering what Saturdays were like then. I sat down to drink my coffee, and the Lord spoke to me. It was as if He said, "OK, are you going to live in the past, or are you going to face today and tomorrow with a different attitude? Are you going to feel sorry for yourself all day, or let it go?" After *much* consideration, I decided to let it go. I need to tell you that I've had to consciously let it go every day since that morning, and I imagine I'll have to let it go every day from now on until God makes my future clear to me.

I began to weep before Him. At first, it was more of a "God, help me, I can't do this myself!" kind of weeping. But as the minutes ticked away, I felt God reach down and scoop me up into His arms and wrap me up in His love with a tenderness that made all my empty feelings pass away. I sensed Him saying, "Let it go, child, I'm here. I'm all you need. It's going to be all right." It was an incredible feeling. I've often thought, since the divorce, that the worst thing about being single after years of having a spouse is that you no longer hear those words, "I love you." Knowing another human being loves you is a need we all have, but God let me know that day that His love for me surpasses that human love by leaps and bounds.

In the Scriptures that day, I found Isaiah 41:10-20. Here are some jewels from that text:

> You are my servant, I have chosen you, and not cast you away. Fear not, for I am with you. Be not dismayed, for I am your God. I will strengthen you, yes, I will help

you; I will uphold you with my righteous right hand.
. . . The poor and needy seek water, but there is none.
Their tongues fail for thirst. I, the Lord, will hear them
. . . I will open rivers in desolate heights, and fountains
in the midst of valleys; I will make the wilderness a
pool of water and the dry land springs of water . . . I
will plant in the wilderness the cedar and acacia tree,
and the box tree together, that they may see and know
and consider and understand together, that the hand of
the Lord has done this, and the Holy One of Israel has
created it.

It was an answer to my questioning heart that day that He knew exactly how I felt, and once again, He would not leave me. He'd "chosen" me to love, and in the midst of this dry desert wilderness that I found myself living in, He would give me a river to refresh my thirsting heart. The trees referred to in this text spoke to me of how He will start a new growth of ministry in my life, and that when it comes to fruition, as a tree does, people will know that it's only God who could have done it!

Later that day, I had to do some shopping to return an item. As I was talking to the salesperson, I heard someone say my name. I turned to find a former neighbor standing there. It wasn't just any former neighbor—we'd been good friends when my ex and I had lived in our old neighborhood. My two kids were the same ages as hers, and I had served as their babysitter for a couple of years when I was a stay-at-home mom. We'd grown to be good friends in those years. For a while after we'd moved to our new house, we'd stayed in touch with each other. Busy schedules and activities had eventually separated us, but somehow you never forget those people with whom you've shared so much. We embraced. It's funny how years can melt away in a moment, and feelings of closeness can come to the surface so quickly with someone who was once a part of our lives. After a few moments of small talk, we got down to the basics.

I shared my loss of my marriage; she shared her loss of her husband to cancer less than a year before. We were equally saddened, and it became harder to hold back the tears as we talked. I talked of the pain of being abandoned. She spoke of the pain of watching her husband lose his five-year battle with a disease that, in the end, couldn't be beaten.

We talked about our kids. We talked about how quickly life changes. Mainly we talked about the loneliness. It was a small miracle that brought us to that place at the same time that day. She told me that she never shopped in that store. I, in turn, told her of all the delays I'd had that day that led me get to that very same store at just that particular moment. We both knew it was no accident. This was God.

We exchanged phone numbers, said our goodbyes, and went our separate ways. I for one, will always cherish those moments we shared together. I believe God was letting us both know that we may feel lonely, but we're not alone. He was showing us both that He cares enough for us to send one person into the path of the other as a reminder of that love and how important we are to His heart.

God's love for us is so incredible. Sometimes, when things happen, we forget that. He loves me enough to know better than I do what my own personal "finished product" will be. I'm growing. I'm changing, just as my circumstances change. I'm constantly learning.

Why do we so often think that learning is only for the young?

Growth hurts. I remember getting terrible leg cramps at night when I was a young girl. Some were due to the sickness I had, but even after my sickness passed, I still had them occasionally. I remember my mother telling me they were just "growing pains."

The pain from my divorce was no different—and the solution was the same. Instead of looking at my temporary pain—and it *was* temporary—I decided to look to the One who knows me better than anyone else. I chose to believe He's got my future under control, and He will complete the work He began forty-three years ago in that younger version of me setting out to college for the first time. May He help me to keep that eagerness to tackle the world that I had then!

I'm amazed at all the things that have changed since then. I'm amazed at how I've changed and grown. I know God's not through with me yet, but I sense something on the horizon that I didn't in the beginning of all of this. There's a hopeful expectation now that didn't exist then. I'm anticipating God's promises He's made to me again, as I also admit I'd lost the vision for them back when I began this journey. I can't wait to see Him complete the work in me. This has been a detour I didn't anticipate or ask for, but because of it, God's begun to equip me for whatever it is He's planned for me. I know it's made me stronger.

My life is not the only one that has changed. My children have grown, too. I'm happy for the people that He's brought into their lives to be partners with them. I need only to look to my daughter's marriage to see how good God is to us: He's given her a wonderful man who loves God, her, and my grandson in an amazing way that I could never have even dreamed possible. They now have a little daughter together as well. Megan calls her husband her "warrior" because, she said, "He fought for me." She's right—and I'm looking forward to what God is going to do in their lives and in their future. It's that very answer to my prayers that makes me so sure that God has plans for me too, and for all of us, if we just remain strong and faithful.

God is doing great things in my son and daughter-in-law's lives as well, and I'm grateful for God's goodness to them. They now have three children, and God is using Ben and Ashley in music ministry as well as in the restaurant business. When I think of the hurts my son felt during and after the time his dad left us, I'm thankful for God's healing power. I can see the spiritual growth, and I know God has done a great work there. He's matured in ways that I never expected, and I'm excited to think of what the future might hold for him and his family.

At this point in my journey, I know that I'm truly blessed. I'm doing my best to look forward, not backwards, and that's important in order to be open to whatever God has in store for me. He's helped me through all the steps needed to be completely healed of the hurts from my broken relationship with my ex-husband. I know there will be setbacks, for I am only human. But at this moment, right now, I feel so much freer than I ever thought I would feel!

God is helping me find my way again after such a devastating loss. I have my eyes peeled on the path before me, not looking behind, and I can't wait to discover what's ahead!

Here are some scriptures that I have found particularly helpful as I continue to seek God's will for my future. I hope you find them helpful in your journey, as well.

> I wait for the Lord, my soul waits, and in His Word I do hope.
> —Psa. 130:5

> If any of you lacks wisdom, let him ask of God, who gives to all liberally, and without reproach, and it will be given to him.
> —Jam. 1:5

> I will instruct you and teach you in the way that you should go; I will guide you with My eye.
> —Psa. 32:8

> Your ear shall hear a word behind you saying, "This is the way, walk in it," whenever you turn to the right hand or whenever you turn to the left.
> —Isa. 30:21

> The steps of a good man [or woman!] are ordered by the Lord, and He delights in his way.
> —Psa. 37:23

FOLLOW THE PATH

Trust in the Lord with all your heart, and lean not on your own understanding; in all your ways acknowledge Him, and He shall direct your path.

—Prov. 3:5, 6

Thus says the Lord your Redeemer, the Holy One of Israel: "I am the Lord your God, who teaches you to profit, who leads you by the way you should go."

—Isa. 48:17

My soul, wait silently for God alone, for my expectation is from Him.

—Psa. 62:5

Let us hold fast the confession of our hope without wavering, for He who promised is faithful.

—Heb. 10:23

The eyes of all look expectantly to You, and You give them food in due season. You open Your hand and satisfy the desire of every living thing.

—Psa. 145:15, 16

www.ingramcontent.com/pod-product-compliance
Lightning Source LLC
LaVergne TN
LVHW051524070426
835507LV00023B/3298